This is a technical explanation of the Convention between the United States and the Republic of Slovenia signed on June 21, 1999 (the "Convention").

Negotiations took into account the U.S. Treasury Department's current tax treaty policy, and the U.S. Treasury Department's Model Income Tax Convention published on September 30, 1996. Negotiations also took into account the Model Tax Convention on Income and on Capital, published by the Organization for Economic Cooperation and Development, as updated in November, 1997 (the "OECD Model") and recent tax treaties concluded by both countries.

The Technical Explanation is an official guide to the Convention. It reflects the policies behind particular Convention provisions, as well as understandings reached with respect to the application and interpretation of the Convention. References in the Technical Explanation to "he" or "his" should be read to mean "he or she" or "his or her".

ARTICLE 1 (GENERAL SCOPE)

Paragraph 1

Paragraph 1 of Article 1 provides that the Convention applies to residents of the United States or Slovenia except where the terms of the Convention provide otherwise. Under Article 4 (Residence) a person is generally treated as a resident of a Contracting State if that person is, under the laws of that State, liable to tax therein by reason of his domicile, residence or other similar criteria. If, however, a person is considered a resident of both Contracting States, Article 4 provides rules for determining a single state of residence (or no state of residence). This determination governs for all purposes of the Convention.

Certain provisions are applicable to persons who may not be residents of either Contracting State. For example, Article 19 (Government Service) may apply to an employee of a Contracting State who is resident in neither State. Paragraph 1 of Article 24 (Non-Discrimination) applies to nationals of the Contracting States. Under Article 26 (Exchange of Information and Administrative Assistance), information may be exchanged with respect to residents of third states.

Paragraph 2

Paragraph 2 states the generally accepted relationship both between the Convention and domestic law and between the Convention and other agreements between the Contracting States (i.e., that no provision in the Convention may restrict any benefit accorded by the tax laws of the Contracting States, or by any other agreement between the Contracting States). The list in paragraph 2 contains examples of benefits not to be restricted and is not intended to be exhaustive.

For example, if a deduction would be allowed under the U.S. Internal Revenue Code (the "Code") in computing the U.S. taxable income of a resident of Slovenia, the deduction also is allowed to that person in computing taxable income under the Convention. Paragraph 2 also means that the Convention may not increase the tax burden on a resident of a Contracting State beyond the burden determined under domestic law. Thus, a right to tax given by the Convention cannot be exercised unless that right also exists under internal law. The relationship between the non-discrimination provisions of the Convention and other agreements is not addressed in paragraph 2 but in paragraph 3.

It follows that under the principle of paragraph 2 a taxpayer's liability to U.S. tax need not be determined under the Convention if the Code would produce a more favorable result. A taxpayer may not, however, choose among the provisions of the Code and the Convention in an inconsistent manner in order to minimize tax. For example, assume that a resident of Slovenia has three separate businesses in the United States. One is a profitable permanent establishment and the other two are trades or businesses that would earn taxable income under the Code but that do not meet the permanent establishment threshold tests of the Convention. One is profitable and the other incurs a loss. Under the Convention, the income of the permanent establishment is taxable, and both the profit and loss of the other two businesses are ignored. Under the Code, all three would be subject to tax, but the loss would be offset against the profits of the two profitable ventures. The taxpayer may not invoke the Convention to exclude the profits of the profitable trade or business and invoke the Code to claim the loss of the loss trade or business against the profit of the permanent establishment. (See Rev. Rul. 84-17, 1984-1 C.B. 308.) If, however, the taxpayer invokes the Code for the taxation of all three ventures, he would not be precluded from invoking the Convention with respect, for example, to any dividend income he may receive from the United States that is not effectively connected with any of his business activities in the United States.

Similarly, nothing in the Convention can be used to deny any benefit granted by any other agreement between the United States and Slovenia. For example, if certain benefits are provided for diplomats under a consular convention between the United States and Slovenia, those benefits or protections will be available to residents of the Contracting State, regardless of any provisions to the contrary (or silence) in the Convention.

Paragraph 3

Paragraph 3 specifically relates to non-discrimination obligations of the Contracting States under other agreements. The provisions of paragraph 3 are an exception to the rule provided in paragraph 2 of this Article under which the Convention shall not restrict in any manner any benefit now or hereafter accorded by any other agreement between the Contracting States.

Subparagraph (a) of paragraph 3 provides that, notwithstanding any other agreement to which the Contracting States may be parties, a dispute concerning whether a measure is within the scope of this Convention shall be considered only by the competent authorities of the Contracting States, and the procedures under this Convention exclusively shall apply to the dispute. Thus, procedures for dealing with disputes that may be incorporated into trade, investment, or other agreements between the Contracting States shall not apply for the purpose of determining the scope of the Convention.

Subparagraph (b) of paragraph 3 provides that, unless the competent authorities determine that a taxation measure is not within the scope of this Convention, the non-discrimination obligations of this Convention exclusively shall apply with respect to that measure, except for such national treatment or most-favored-nation ("MFN") obligations as may apply to trade in goods under the General Agreement on Tariffs and Trade ("GATT"). No national treatment or MFN obligation under any other agreement shall apply with respect to that measure. Thus, unless the competent authorities agree otherwise, any national treatment and MFN obligations undertaken by the Contracting States under agreements other than the Convention shall not apply to a taxation measure, with the exception of GATT as applicable to trade in goods.

Subparagraph (c) of paragraph 3 defines a "measure" broadly. It would include, for example, a law, regulation, rule, procedure, decision, administrative action or guidance, or any other form of governmental action or guidance.

Paragraph 4

Paragraph 4 contains the traditional saving clause found in U.S. tax treaties. The Contracting States reserve their rights, except as provided in paragraph 5, to tax their residents and citizens as provided in their internal laws, notwithstanding any provisions of the Convention to the contrary. For example, if a resident of Slovenia performs independent personal services in the United States and the income from the services is not attributable to a fixed base in the United States, Article 14 (Independent Personal Services) would by its terms prevent the United States from taxing the income. If, however, the resident of Slovenia is also a citizen of the United States, the saving clause permits the United States to include the remuneration in the worldwide income of the citizen and subject it to tax under the normal Code rules (i.e., without regard to Code section 894(a)). However, paragraph 5(a) of this Article preserves the benefits of special foreign tax credit rules applicable to the U.S. taxation of certain U.S. income of its citizens resident in Slovenia. See paragraph 3 of Article 23 (Relief from Double Taxation).

For purposes of the saving clause, "residence" is determined under Article 4 (Residence). Thus, if an individual who is not a U.S. citizen is a resident of the United States under the Code, and is also a resident of Slovenia under its law, and that individual has a permanent home available to him in Slovenia and not in the United States, he would be treated as a resident of Slovenia under Article 4 and for purposes of the saving clause. The United States would not be permitted to apply its statutory rules to that person if they are inconsistent with the treaty. Thus, an individual who is a U.S. resident under the Internal Revenue Code but who is deemed to be a resident of Slovenia under the tie-breaker rules of Article 4 (Residence) would be subject to U.S. tax only to the extent permitted by the Convention. However, the person would be treated as a U.S. resident for U.S. tax purposes other than determining the individual's U.S. tax liability. For example, in determining under Code section 957 whether a foreign corporation is a controlled foreign corporation, shares in that corporation held by the individual would be considered to be held by a U.S. resident. As a result, other U.S. citizens or residents might be deemed to be United States shareholders of a controlled foreign corporation subject to current inclusion of Subpart F income recognized by the corporation. See Treas. Reg. section 301.7701(b)-7(a)(3).

Under paragraph 4 each Contracting State also reserves its right to tax former citizens and long-term residents whose loss of citizenship or long-term residence had as one of its principal purposes the avoidance of tax. The United States generally treats an individual as having a principal purpose to avoid tax if (a) the average annual net income tax of such individual for the period of 5 taxable years ending before the date of the loss of status is greater than $100,000, or (b) the net worth of such individual as of such date is $500,000 or more. The United States defines "long-term resident" as an individual (other than a U.S. citizen) who is a lawful permanent resident of the United States in at least 8 of the prior 15 taxable years. An individual shall not be treated as a lawful permanent resident for any taxable year if such individual is treated as a resident of a foreign country under the provisions of a tax treaty between the United States and the foreign country and the individual does not waive the benefits of such treaty applicable to residents of the foreign country. In the United States, such a former citizen or long-term resident is taxable in accordance with the provisions of section 877 of the Code.

Paragraph 5

Some provisions are intended to provide benefits to citizens and residents even if such benefits do not exist under internal law. Paragraph 5 sets forth certain exceptions to the saving clause that preserve these benefits for citizens and residents of the Contracting States. Sub-paragraph (a) lists certain provisions of the Convention that are applicable to all citizens and residents of a Contracting State, despite the general saving clause rule of paragraph 4: (1) Paragraph 2 of Article 9 (Associated Enterprises) grants the right to a correlative adjustment with respect to income tax due on profits reallocated under Article 9. (2) Paragraphs 2 and 5 of Article 18 (Pensions, Social Security, Annuities, Alimony and Child Support) deal with social security benefits and child support payments, respectively. The inclusion of paragraph 2 in the exceptions to the saving clause means that the grant of exclusive taxing right of social security benefits to the paying country applies to deny, for example, to the United States the right to tax its citizens and residents on social security benefits paid by the Republic of Slovenia. The inclusion of paragraph 5, which exempts child support payments from taxation by the State of residence of the recipient, means that if a resident of Slovenia pays child support to a citizen or resident of the United States, the United States may not tax the recipient. (3) Article 23 (Relief from Double Taxation) confirms the benefit of a credit to citizens and residents of one Contracting State for income taxes paid to the other. (4) Article 24 (Non-Discrimination) requires one Contracting State to grant national treatment to residents and citizens of the other Contracting State in certain circumstances. Excepting this Article from the saving clause requires, for example, that the United States give such benefits to a resident or citizen of Slovenia even if that person is a citizen of the United States. (5) Article 25 (Mutual Agreement Procedure) may confer benefits on citizens and residents of the Contracting States. For example, the statute of limitations may be waived for refunds and the competent authorities are permitted to use a definition of a term that differs from the internal law definition. As with the foreign tax credit, these benefits are intended to be granted by a Contracting State to its citizens and residents.

Subparagraph (b) of paragraph 5 provides a different set of exceptions to the saving clause. The benefits referred to are all intended to be granted to temporary residents of a Contracting State (for example, in the case of the United States, holders of non-immigrant visas), but not to citizens or to persons who have acquired permanent residence in that State. If beneficiaries of these provisions travel from one of the Contracting States to the other, and remain in the other long enough to become residents under its internal law, but do not acquire permanent residence status (i.e., in the U.S. context, they do not become "green card" holders) and are not citizens of that State, the host State will continue to grant these benefits even if they conflict with the statutory rules. The benefits preserved by this paragraph are the host country exemptions for the following items: government service salaries and pensions under Article 19 (Government Service); certain income of visiting students, trainees, professors, and researchers under Article 20 (Students, Trainees, Professors, and Researchers); and the income of diplomatic agents and consular officers under Article 27 (Diplomatic Agents and Consular Officers).

ARTICLE 2 (TAXES COVERED)

This Article specifies the U.S. taxes and the Slovenian taxes to which the Convention applies. With two exceptions, the taxes specified in Article 2 are the covered taxes for all purposes of the Convention. A broader coverage applies, however, for purposes of Articles 2 (Non-discrimination) and 26 (Exchange of Information and Administrative Assistance). Article 24 applies with respect to all taxes, including those imposed by state and local governments. Article 26 applies with respect to all taxes imposed at the national level.

Paragraph 1

Subparagraph 1(a) provides that the United States covered taxes are the Federal income taxes imposed by the Code, together with the excise taxes imposed with respect to private foundations (Code sections 4940 through 4948). Although they may be regarded as income taxes, social security taxes (Code sections 1401, 3101, 3111 and 3301) are specifically excluded from coverage. It is expected that social security taxes will be dealt with in bilateral Social Security Totalization Agreements, which are negotiated and administered by the Social Security Administration. Except with respect to Article 24 (Non-Discrimination), state and local taxes in the United States are not covered by the Convention.

In this Convention, like the U.S. Model, but unlike some U.S. treaties, the Accumulated Earnings Tax and the Personal Holding Companies Tax are covered taxes because they are income taxes and they are not otherwise excluded from coverage. Under the Code, these taxes will not apply to most foreign corporations because of a statutory exclusion or the corporation's failure to meet a statutory requirement.

Subparagraph 1(b) specifies the existing taxes of Slovenia that are covered by the Convention. They are the tax on profits of legal persons, the tax on income of individuals, and the assets tax on banks and savings institutions.

Paragraph 2

Under paragraph 2, the Convention will apply to any taxes that are identical, or substantially similar, to those enumerated in paragraph 1, and which are imposed in addition to, or in place of, the existing taxes after the date of signature of the Convention. The paragraph also provides that the competent authorities of the Contracting States will notify each other of significant changes in their taxation laws or of other laws that affect their obligations under the Convention. The use of the term "significant" means that changes must be reported that are of significance to the operation of the Convention. Other laws that may affect a Contracting State's obligations under the Convention may include, for example, laws affecting bank secrecy.

The competent authorities are also obligated to notify each other of official published materials concerning the application of the Convention. This requirement encompasses materials such as technical explanations, regulations, rulings and judicial decisions relating to the Convention.

ARTICLE 3 (GENERAL DEFINITIONS)

Paragraph 1

Paragraph 1 defines a number of basic terms used in the Convention. Certain others are defined in other articles of the Convention. For example, the term "resident of a Contracting State" is defined in Article 4 (Residence). The term "permanent establishment" is defined in Article 5 (Permanent Establishment). The terms "dividends," "interest" and "royalties" are defined in Articles 10, 11 and 12, respectively. The introduction to paragraph 1 makes clear that these definitions apply for all purposes of the Convention, unless the context requires otherwise. This latter condition allows flexibility in the interpretation of the treaty in order to avoid unintended results. Terms that are not defined in the Convention are dealt with in paragraph 2.

Subparagraph 1(a) defines the term "person" to include an individual, an estate, a trust, a partnership, a company and any other body of persons. The definition is significant for a variety of reasons. For example, under Article 4, only a "person" can be a "resident" and therefore eligible for most benefits under the treaty. Also, all "persons" are eligible to claim relief under Article 25 (Mutual Agreement Procedure).

The term "company" is defined in subparagraph 1(b) as a body corporate or an entity treated as a body corporate for tax purposes in the state where it is organized.

The terms "enterprise of a Contracting State" and "enterprise of the other Contracting State" are defined in subparagraph 1(c) as an enterprise carried on by a resident of a Contracting State and an enterprise carried on by a resident of the other Contracting State. The term "enterprise" is not defined in the Convention, nor is it defined in the OECD Model or its Commentaries. Despite the absence of a clear, generally accepted meaning for the term "enterprise," the term is understood to refer to any activity or set of activities that constitute a trade or business.

An enterprise of a Contracting State need not be carried on in that State. It may be carried on in the other Contracting State or a third state (e.g., a U.S. corporation doing all of its business in Slovenia would still be a U.S. enterprise).

Subparagraph 1(d) defines the term "international traffic." The term means any transport by a ship or aircraft except when the transport is solely between places within a Contracting State. This definition is applicable principally in the context of Article 8 (Shipping and Air Transport). The definition combines with paragraphs 2 and 3 of Article 8 to exempt from tax by the source State income from the rental of ships, aircraft or containers that is earned both by lessors that are operators of ships and aircraft and by those lessors that are not (e.g., banks or container leasing companies).

The exclusion from international traffic of transport solely between places within a Contracting State means, for example, that carriage of goods or passengers solely between New York and Chicago would not be treated as international traffic, whether carried by a U.S. or a foreign carrier. The substantive taxing rules of the Convention relating to the taxation of income from transport, principally Article 8 (Shipping and Air Transport), therefore, would not apply to income from such carriage. Thus, if the carrier engaged in internal U.S. traffic were a resident of Slovenia (assuming that were possible under U.S. law), the United States would not be required to exempt the income from that transport under Article 8. The income would, however, be treated as business profits under Article 7 (Business Profits), and therefore would be taxable in the United States only if attributable to a U.S. permanent establishment of the foreign carrier, and then only on a net basis. The gross basis U.S. tax imposed by section 887 would never apply under the circumstances described. If, however, goods or passengers are carried by a carrier resident in Slovenia from a non-U.S. port to, for example, New York, and some of the goods or passengers continue on to Chicago, the entire transport would be international traffic. This would be true if the international carrier transferred the goods at the U.S. port of entry from a ship to a land vehicle, from a ship to a lighter, or even if the overland portion of the trip in the United States was handled by an independent carrier under contract with the original international carrier, so long as both parts of the trip were reflected in original bills of lading. For this reason, the Convention refers, in the definition of "international traffic," to "such transport" being solely between places in a Contracting State, while the OECD Model refers to the ship or aircraft being operated solely between such places. The definition is intended to make clear that, as in the above example, even if the goods are carried on a different aircraft for the internal portion of the international voyage than is used for the overseas portion of the trip, the definition applies to that internal portion as well as the external portion.

Finally, a "cruise to nowhere," i.e., a cruise beginning and ending in a port in the same Contracting State with no stops in a foreign port, would not constitute international traffic.

Subparagraphs 1(e)(i) and (ii) define the term "competent authority" for the United States and Slovenia respectively. The U.S. competent authority is the Secretary of the Treasury or his delegate. The Secretary of the Treasury has delegated the competent authority function to the Commissioner of Internal Revenue, who in turn has delegated the authority to the Assistant Commissioner (International). With respect to interpretative issues, the Assistant Commissioner acts with the concurrence of the Associate Chief Counsel (International) of the Internal Revenue Service. The Slovenian competent authority is the Ministry of Finance, or his authorized representative.

The term "United States" is defined in subparagraph 1(f) to mean the United States of America, including the states, the District of Columbia and the territorial sea of the United States. The term does not include Puerto Rico, the Virgin Islands, Guam or any other U.S. possession or territory. The geographical meaning of the term United States also includes the territorial sea of the United States, and for certain purposes, the definition is extended to include the sea bed and subsoil of undersea areas adjacent to the territorial sea of the United States. This extension applies to the extent that the United States exercises sovereignty in accordance with international law for the purpose of natural resource exploration and exploitation of such areas. This extension of the definition applies, however, only if the person, property or activity to which the Convention is being applied is connected with such natural resource exploration or exploitation. Thus, it would not include any activity involving the sea floor of an area over which the United States exercised sovereignty for natural resource purposes if that activity was unrelated to the exploration and exploitation of natural resources.

The term "Slovenia" is defined in subparagraph 1(g) to mean the Republic of Slovenia, and, when used in a geographical sense, the territory of the Republic of Slovenia, including the territorial sea, sea bed and subsoil adjacent to the territorial sea to the extent the Republic of

Slovenia exercises its sovereign rights or jurisdiction over such territorial sea, sea area, sea bed and subsoil in accordance with its domestic legislation and international law.

The term "national," as it relates to the United States and to Slovenia, is defined in subparagraphs l(h)(i) and (ii). This term is relevant for purposes of Articles 19 (Government Service) and 24 (Non-Discrimination). A national of one of the Contracting States is (1) an individual who is a citizen or national of that State, and (2) any legal person, partnership or association deriving its status as such from the law in force in the State where it is established.

The definition of the term "qualified governmental entity" in subparagraph 1(i) is relevant for purposes of Articles 4 (Residence), Article 10 (Dividends) and 22 (Limitation on Benefits). The term means: (i) the Government of a Contracting State or of a political subdivision or local authority of the Contracting State; (ii) A person wholly owned by a governmental entity described in subparagraph (i), that satisfies certain organizational and funding standards; and (iii) a pension fund of a person that meets the standards of subparagraphs (i) and (ii) and that provides government service pension benefits, described in Article 19 (Government Service). A qualified governmental entity described in either subparagraphs (ii) or (iii) may not engage in any commercial activity.

Paragraph 2

Paragraph 2 provides that in the application of the Convention, any term used but not defined in the Convention will have the meaning that it has under the law of the Contracting State whose tax is being applied, unless the context requires otherwise. The paragraph makes clear that if the term is defined under both the tax and non-tax laws of a Contracting State, the definition in the tax law will take precedence over the definition in the non-tax laws. Finally, there also may be cases where the tax laws of a State contain multiple definitions of the same term. In such a case, the definition used for purposes of the particular provision at issue, if any, should be used.

If the meaning of a term cannot be readily determined under the law of a Contracting State, or if there is a conflict in meaning under the laws of the two States that creates difficulties in the application of the Convention, the competent authorities, as indicated in paragraph 3(f) of Article 25 (Mutual Agreement Procedure), may establish a common meaning in order to prevent double taxation or to further any other purpose of the Convention. This common meaning need not conform to the meaning of the term under the laws of either Contracting State.

The reference in paragraph 2 to the internal law of a Contracting State means the law in effect at the time the treaty is being applied, not the law as in effect at the time the treaty was signed. The use of "ambulatory" definitions, however, may lead to results that are at variance with the intentions of the negotiators and of the Contracting States when the treaty was negotiated and ratified. The reference in both paragraphs 1 and 2 to the "context otherwise requiring" a definition different from the treaty definition, in paragraph 1, or from the internal law definition of the Contracting State whose tax is being imposed, under paragraph 2, refers to a circumstance where the result intended by the Contracting States is different from the result that would obtain under either the paragraph 1 definition or the statutory definition. Thus, flexibility in defining terms is necessary and permitted.

ARTICLE 4 (RESIDENCE)

This Article sets forth rules for determining whether a person is a resident of a Contracting State for purposes of the Convention. As a general matter only residents of the Contracting States may claim the benefits of the Convention. The treaty definition of residence is to be used only for purposes of the Convention. The fact that a person is determined to be a resident of a Contracting State under Article 4 does not necessarily entitle that person to the benefits of the Convention. In addition to being a resident, a person also must qualify for benefits under Article 22 (Limitation on Benefits) in order to receive benefits conferred on residents of a Contracting State.

The determination of residence for treaty purposes looks first to a person's liability to tax as a resident under the respective taxation laws of the Contracting States. As a general matter, a person who, under those laws, is a resident of one Contracting State and not of the other need look no further. For purposes of the Convention, that person is a resident of the State in which he is resident under internal law. If, however, a person is resident in both Contracting States under their respective taxation laws, the Article proceeds, where possible, to use tie-breaker rules to assign a single State of residence to such a person for purposes of the Convention.

Paragraph 1

The term "resident of a Contracting State" is defined in paragraph 1. In general, this definition incorporates the definitions of residence in U.S. and Slovenian law by referring to a resident as a person who, under the laws of a Contracting State, is subject to tax there by reason of his domicile, residence, citizenship, place of management, place of incorporation or any other similar criterion. Thus, residents of the United States include aliens who are considered U.S. residents under Code section 7701(b). Subparagraphs (a) through (d) each address special cases that may arise in the context of Article 4.

Notwithstanding the general rule, the introductory language in paragraph 1 also provides that a U.S. citizen or alien lawfully admitted for permanent residence (i.e., a "green card" holder) will be treated as a resident of the United States for purposes of the Convention, and, thereby entitled to treaty benefits, only if he has a substantial presence (see section 7701(b)(3)), permanent home or habitual abode in the United States. If such a person is a resident both of the United States and Slovenia, whether or not he is to be treated as a resident of the United States for purposes of the Convention is determined by the tie-breaker rules of paragraph 2. If, however, he is resident in the United States and not Slovenia but has ties to a third State, in the absence of the Protocol subparagraph he would always be a resident of the United States, no matter how tenuous his relationship with the United States relative to that with the third State.

Thus, for example, an individual resident of Mexico who is a U.S. citizen by birth, or who is a Mexican citizen and holds a U.S. green card, but who, in either case, has never lived in the United States, would not be entitled to Slovenian benefits under the Convention. On the other hand, a U.S. citizen employed by a U.S. corporation who is transferred to Mexico for two years but who maintains a permanent home or habitual abode in the United States would be entitled to treaty benefits. The fact that a U.S. citizen who does not have close ties to the United States may not be treated as a U.S. resident under the Convention does not alter the application of the saving clause of paragraph 4 of Article 1 (General Scope) to that citizen. For example, a U.S. citizen who pursuant to the "citizen/green card holder" rule is not considered to be a resident of the United States still is taxable on his worldwide income under the generally applicable rules of the Code.

Certain entities that are nominally subject to tax but that in practice rarely pay tax also would generally be treated as residents and therefore accorded treaty benefits. For example, RICs, REITs and REMICs are all residents of the United States for purposes of the treaty. Although the income earned by these entities normally is not subject to U.S. tax in the hands of the entity, they are taxable to the extent that they do not currently distribute their profits, and therefore may be regarded as "liable to tax." They also must satisfy a number of requirements under the Code in order to be entitled to special tax treatment.

Subparagraph (a) provides that a person who is liable to tax in a Contracting State only in respect of income from sources within that State or capital situated therein or of profits attributable to a permanent establishment in that State will not be treated as a resident of that Contracting State for purposes of the Convention. Thus, a consular official of Slovenia who is posted in the United States, who may be subject to U.S. tax on U.S. source investment income, but is not taxable in the United States on non-U.S. source income, would not be considered a resident of the United States for purposes of the Convention. (See Code section 7701(b)(5)(B)). Similarly, an enterprise of Slovenia with a permanent establishment in the United States is not, by virtue of that permanent establishment, a resident of the United States. The enterprise generally is subject to U.S. tax only with respect to its income that is attributable to the U.S. permanent establishment, not with respect to its worldwide income, as it would be if it were a U.S. resident.

Subparagraph (b) addresses special issues presented by fiscally transparent entities such as partnerships and certain estates and trusts. In general, subparagraph (b) relates to entities that are not subject to tax at the entity level. This subparagraph applies to any resident of a Contracting State who is entitled to income derived through an entity that is treated as fiscally transparent under the laws of either Contracting State. Entities falling under this description in the United States would include partnerships, common investment trusts under section 584 and grantor trusts. This paragraph also applies to U.S. limited liability companies ("LLC"s) that are treated as partnerships for U.S. tax purposes. Under current Slovenian law, all entities are subject to tax at the entity level. Accordingly, under current Slovenian law, no entity falls under this description of fiscal transparency.

Subparagraph (b) provides that an item of income derived by such a fiscally transparent entity will be considered to be derived by a resident of a Contracting State if the resident is treated under the taxation laws of the State where he is resident as deriving the item of income. For example, if a Slovenian corporation distributes a dividend to an entity that is treated as fiscally transparent for U.S. tax purposes, the dividend will be considered derived by a resident of the United States only to the extent that the taxation laws of the United States treat one or more U.S. residents (whose status as U.S. residents is determined, for this purpose, under U.S. tax laws) as deriving the dividend income for U.S. tax purposes. In the case of a partnership, the persons who are, under U.S. tax laws, treated as partners of the entity would normally be the persons whom the U.S. tax laws would treat as deriving the dividend income through the partnership. Also, it follows that persons whom the U.S. treats as partners but who are not U.S. residents for U.S. tax purposes may not claim a benefit for the dividend paid to the entity under the Convention, because they are not residents of the United States for purposes of claiming this treaty benefit. (If, however, the country in which they are treated as resident for tax purposes, as determined under the laws of that country, has an income tax convention with Slovenia, they may be entitled to claim a benefit under that convention). In contrast, if, for example, an entity is organized under U.S. laws and is classified as a corporation for U.S. tax purposes, dividends paid by a Slovenian corporation to the U.S. entity will be considered derived by a resident of the United States since the U.S. corporation is treated under U.S. taxation laws as a resident of the United States and as deriving the income.

These results would obtain even if the entity were viewed differently under the tax laws of Slovenia (e.g., as not fiscally transparent in the first example above where the entity is treated as a partnership for U.S. tax purposes). Similarly, the characterization of the entity in a third country is also irrelevant, even if the entity is organized in that third country. The results follow regardless of whether the entity is disregarded as a separate entity under the laws of one jurisdiction but not the other, such as a single owner entity that is viewed as a branch for U.S. tax purposes and as a corporation for Slovenian tax purposes. These results also obtain regardless of where the entity is organized, i.e., in the United States, Slovenia, or in a third country.

For example, income from U.S. sources received by an entity organized under the laws of the U.S., which is treated for Slovenian tax purposes as a corporation and is owned by a Slovenian shareholder who is a Slovenian resident for Slovenian tax purposes, is not considered derived by the shareholder of that corporation even if, under the tax laws of the U.S., the entity is treated as fiscally transparent. Rather, for purposes of the treaty, the income is treated as derived by the U.S. entity.

These principles also apply to trusts to the extent that they are fiscally transparent in either Contracting State. For example, if X, a resident of Slovenia, creates a revocable trust and names persons resident in a third country as the beneficiaries of the trust, X would be treated as the beneficial owner of income derived from the United States under the Code's rules. If Slovenia has no rules comparable to those in sections 671 through 679 of the Code, then it is possible that under Slovenian law neither X nor the trust would be taxed on the income derived from the

United States. In these cases, it is to be understood that the trust's income would be regarded as being derived by a resident of Slovenia only to the extent that the laws of Slovenia treat Slovenian residents as deriving the income for tax purposes.

The taxation laws of a Contracting State may treat an item of income, profit or gain as income, profit or gain of a resident of that State even if, under the taxation laws of that State, the resident is not subject to tax on that particular item of income, profit or gain. For example, if a Contracting State has a participation exemption for certain foreign-source dividends and capital gains, such income or gains would be regarded as income or gain of a resident of that State who otherwise derived the income or gain, despite the fact that the resident could be exempt from tax in that State on the income or gain.

Income is derived through a fiscally transparent entity if the entity's participation in the transaction giving rise to the income, profit or gain in question is respected after application of any source State anti-abuse principles based on substance over form and similar analyses. For example, if a partnership with U.S. partners receives income arising in Slovenia, that income will be considered to be derived through the partnership by its partners as long as the partnership's participation in the transaction is not disregarded for lack of economic substance. In such a case, the partners would be considered to be the beneficial owners of the income.

Subparagraph (c) provides that certain tax-exempt entities such as pension funds and charitable organizations will be regarded as residents of a Contracting State regardless of whether they are generally liable for income tax in the State where they are established. An entity will be described in this subparagraph if it is generally exempt from tax by reason of the fact that it is organized and operated exclusively to perform a charitable or similar purpose or to provide pension or similar benefits to employees pursuant to a plan. The reference to "similar benefits" is intended to encompass employee benefits such as health and disability benefits.

The inclusion of this provision is intended to clarify the generally accepted practice of treating an entity that would be liable for tax as a resident under the internal law of a State but for a specific exemption from tax (either complete or partial) as a resident of that state for purposes of paragraph 1. The reference to a "general" exemption is intended to reflect the fact that under U.S. law, certain organizations that generally are considered to be tax-exempt entities may be subject to certain excise taxes or to income tax on their unrelated business income. Thus, a U.S. pension trust, or an exempt section 501(c) organization (such as a U.S. charity) that is generally exempt from tax under U.S. law is considered a resident of the United States for all purposes of the treaty.

Subparagraph (d) specifies that a qualified governmental entity (as defined in Article 3) established in a Contracting State is to be treated as a resident of that State.

Paragraph 2

If, under the laws of the two Contracting States, and, thus, under paragraph 1, an individual is deemed to be a resident of both Contracting States, a series of tie-breaker rules are provided in paragraph 2 to determine a single State of residence for that individual. These tests are to be applied in the order in which they are stated. The first test is based on where the individual has a permanent home. If that test is inconclusive because the individual has a permanent home available to him in both States, he will be considered to be a resident of the Contracting State where his personal and economic relations are closest (i.e., the location of his "center of vital interests"). If that test is also inconclusive, or if he does not have a permanent home available to him in either State, he will be treated as a resident of the Contracting State where he maintains an habitual abode. If he has an habitual abode in both States or in neither of them, he will be treated as a resident of the Contracting State of which he is a national. If he is a national of both States or of neither, the matter will be considered by the competent authorities, who will assign a single State of residence.

Paragraph 3

Paragraph 3 seeks to settle dual-residence issues for companies. If a company is resident in both the United States and Slovenia under paragraph 1, it will be a resident of the State in which it is created or organized. If, however, it is dual-incorporated, then the competent authorities shall seek to determine a single State of residence for the company for purposes of the Convention. If, however, they are unable to reach agreement, then the company shall not be considered to be a resident of either the United States or Slovenia for purposes of the Convention.

Paragraph 4

Dual residents other than individuals or companies (such as trusts or estates) are addressed by paragraph 4. If such a person is, under the rules of paragraph 1, resident in both Contracting States, the competent authorities shall seek to determine a single State of residence for that person for purposes of the Convention.

ARTICLE 5 (PERMANENT ESTABLISHMENT)

This Article defines the term "permanent establishment," a term that is significant for several articles of the Convention. The existence of a permanent establishment in a Contracting State is necessary under Article 7 (Business Profits) for the taxation by that State of the business profits of a resident of the other Contracting State. Since the term "fixed base" in Article 14 (Independent Personal Services) is understood by reference to the definition of "permanent establishment," this Article is also relevant for purposes of Article 14. Articles 10, 11 and 12 (dealing with dividends, interest, and royalties, respectively) provide for reduced rates of tax at source on payments of these items of income to a resident of the other State only when the income is not attributable to a permanent establishment or fixed base that the recipient has in the source State. The concept is also relevant in determining which Contracting State may tax certain gains under Article 13 (Gains) and certain "other income" under Article 21 (Other Income).

The Article follows closely both the OECD Model and the U.S. Model provisions.

Paragraph 1

The basic definition of the term "permanent establishment" is contained in paragraph 1. As used in the Convention, the term means a fixed place of business through which the business of an enterprise is wholly or partly carried on. As indicated in the OECD Commentaries (see paragraphs 4 through 8), a general principle to be observed in determining whether a permanent establishment exists is that the place of business must be "fixed" in the sense that a particular building or physical location is used by the enterprise for the conduct of its business, and that it must be foreseeable that the enterprise's use of this building or other physical location will be more than temporary.

Paragraph 2

Paragraph 2 lists a number of types of fixed places of business that constitute a permanent establishment. This list is illustrative and non-exclusive. According to paragraph 2, the term permanent establishment includes a place of management, a branch, an office, a factory, a workshop, and a mine, oil or gas well, quarry or other place of extraction of natural resources.

Paragraph 3

This paragraph provides rules to determine whether a building site or a construction or installation project, or an installation or drilling rig or ship used for the exploration of natural resources constitutes a permanent establishment for the contractor, driller, etc. An activity does not create a permanent establishment unless the site, project, etc. lasts or continues for more than twelve months. It is only necessary to refer to "exploration" and not "exploitation" in this context because exploitation activities are defined to constitute a permanent establishment under sub-paragraph (f) of paragraph 2. Thus, a drilling rig does not constitute a permanent establishment if a well is drilled in only six months, but if production begins in the following month the well becomes a permanent establishment as of that date.

The twelve-month test applies separately to each site or project. The twelve-month period begins when work (including preparatory work carried on by the enterprise) physically begins in a Contracting State. A series of contracts or projects by a contractor that are interdependent both commercially and geographically are to be treated as a single project for purposes of applying the twelve-month threshold test. For example, the construction of a housing development would be considered as a single project even if each house were constructed for a different purchaser.

Several drilling rigs operated by a drilling contractor in the same sector of the continental shelf also normally would be treated as a single project.

If the twelve-month threshold is exceeded, the site or project constitutes a permanent establishment from the first day of activity. In applying this paragraph, time spent by a sub-contractor on a building site is counted as time spent by the general contractor at the site for purposes of determining whether the general contractor has a permanent establishment. However, for the sub-contractor itself to be treated as having a permanent establishment, the sub-contractor's activities at the site must last for more than 12 months. If a sub-contractor is on a site intermittently, then, for purposes of applying the 12-month rule, time is measured from the first day the sub-contractor is on the site until the last day (i.e., intervening days that the sub-contractor is not on the site are counted)

These interpretations of the Article are based on the Commentary to paragraph 3 of Article 5 of the OECD Model, which contains language that is substantially the same as that in the Convention (except for the absence in the OECD Model of a rule for drilling rigs). These interpretations are consistent with the generally accepted international interpretation of the relevant language in paragraph 3 of Article 5 of the Convention.

Paragraph 4

This paragraph contains exceptions to the general rule of paragraph 1, listing a number of activities that may be carried on through a fixed place of business, but which nevertheless do not create a permanent establishment. The use of facilities solely to store, display or deliver merchandise belonging to an enterprise does not constitute a permanent establishment of that enterprise. The maintenance of a stock of goods belonging to an enterprise solely for the purpose of storage, display or delivery, or solely for the purpose of processing by another enterprise does not give rise to a permanent establishment of the first-mentioned enterprise. The maintenance of a fixed place of business solely for the purpose of purchasing goods or merchandise, or for collecting information, for the enterprise, or for other activities that have a preparatory or auxiliary character for the enterprise, such as advertising, or the supply of information, do not constitute a permanent establishment of the enterprise. Thus, as explained in paragraph 22 of the OECD Commentaries, a news bureau of a newspaper would not constitute a permanent establishment of the newspaper.

Further, a combination of these activities will not give rise to a permanent establishment: unlike the OECD Model, the Convention provides that the maintenance of a fixed place of business for a combination of the activities listed in subparagraphs (a) through (e) of the paragraph does not give rise to a permanent establishment, without the OECD Model's qualification that the overall combination of activities must be of a preparatory or auxiliary character. The United States position is that a combination of activities that are each preparatory or auxiliary always will result in an overall activity that is also preparatory or auxiliary.

Paragraph 5

Paragraphs 5 and 6 specify when activities carried on by an agent on behalf of an enterprise create a permanent establishment of that enterprise. Under paragraph 5, a dependent agent of an enterprise is deemed to be a permanent establishment of the enterprise if the agent has and habitually exercises an authority to conclude contracts that are binding on the enterprise. If, however, the agent's activities are limited to those activities specified in paragraph 4 which would not constitute a permanent establishment if carried on by the enterprise through a fixed place of business, the agent is not a permanent establishment of the enterprise.

The OECD Model uses the term "in the name of that enterprise" rather than "binding on the enterprise." There is no substantive difference. As indicated in paragraph 32 to the OECD Commentaries on Article 5, paragraph 5 of the Article is intended to encompass a person who "concludes contracts which are binding on the enterprise, even if those contracts are not actually in the name of the enterprise."

The contracts referred to in paragraph 5 are those relating to the essential business operations of the enterprise, rather than ancillary activities. For example, if the agent has no authority to conclude contracts in the name of the enterprise with its customers for, say, the sale of the goods produced by the enterprise, but it can enter into service contracts in the name of the enterprise for the enterprise's business equipment used in the agent's office, this contracting authority would not fall within the scope of the paragraph, even if exercised regularly.

Paragraph 6

Under paragraph 6, an enterprise is not deemed to have a permanent establishment in a Contracting State merely because it carries on business in that State through an independent agent, including a broker or general commission agent, if the agent is acting in the ordinary course of his business as an independent agent. Thus, there are two conditions that must be satisfied: the agent must be both legally and economically independent of the enterprise, and the agent must be acting in the ordinary course of its business in carrying out activities on behalf of the enterprise.

Whether the agent and the enterprise are independent is a factual determination. Among the questions to be considered are the extent to which the agent operates on the basis of instructions from the enterprise. An agent that is subject to detailed instructions regarding the conduct of its operations or comprehensive control by the enterprise is not legally independent.

In determining whether the agent is economically independent, a relevant factor is the extent to which the agent bears business risk. Business risk refers primarily to risk of loss. An independent agent typically bears risk of loss from its own activities. In the absence of other factors that would establish dependence, an agent that shares business risk with the enterprise, or has its own business risk, is economically independent because its business activities are not integrated with those of the principal. Conversely, an agent that bears little or no risk from the activities it performs is not economically independent and therefore is not described in paragraph 6.

Another relevant factor in determining whether an agent is economically independent is whether the agent has an exclusive or nearly exclusive relationship with the principal. Such a relationship may indicate that the principal has economic control over the agent. A number of principals acting in concert also may have economic control over an agent. The limited scope of the agent's activities and the agent's dependence on a single source of income may indicate that the agent lacks economic independence. It should be borne in mind, however, that exclusivity is not in itself a conclusive test: an agent may be economically independent notwithstanding an exclusive relationship with the principal if it has the capacity to diversify and acquire other clients without substantial modifications to its current business and without substantial harm to its business profits. Thus, exclusivity should be viewed merely as a pointer to further investigation of the relationship between the principal and the agent. Each case must be addressed on the basis of its own facts and circumstances.

Paragraph 7

This paragraph clarifies that a company that is a resident of a Contracting State is not deemed to have a permanent establishment in the other Contracting State merely because it controls, or is controlled by, a company that is a resident of that other Contracting State, or that carries on business in that other Contracting State. The determination whether a permanent establishment exists is made solely on the basis of the factors described in paragraphs 1 through 6 of the Article. Whether a company is a permanent establishment of a related company, therefore, is based solely on those factors and not on the ownership or control relationship between the companies.

ARTICLE 6 (INCOME FROM REAL PROPERTY (IMMOVABLE PROPERTY))

Paragraph 1

The first paragraph of Article 6 states the general rule that income of a resident of a Contracting State derived from real property situated in the other Contracting State may be taxed in the Contracting State in which the property is situated. The paragraph specifies that income from real property includes income from agriculture and forestry. Income from agriculture and forestry are dealt with in Article 6 rather than in Article 7 (Business Profits). Given the availability of the net election in paragraph 5, taxpayers generally should be able to obtain the same tax treatment in the situs country regardless of whether the income is treated as business profits or real property income. Paragraph 3 clarifies that the income referred to in paragraph 1 also means income from any use of real property, including, but not limited to, income from direct use by the owner (in which case income may be imputed to the owner for tax purposes) and rental income from the letting of real property.

This Article does not grant an exclusive taxing right to the situs State; the situs State is merely given the primary right to tax. The Article does not impose any limitation in terms of rate or form of tax on the situs State, except that, as provided in paragraph 5, the situs State must allow the taxpayer an election to be taxed on a net basis.

Paragraph 2

The term "real property" ("immovable property") is defined in paragraph 2 by reference to the internal law definition in the situs State. In the case of the United States, the term has the meaning given to it by Reg. § 1.897-1(b). In addition to the statutory definitions in the two Contracting States, the paragraph specifies certain additional classes of property that, regardless of internal law definitions, are to be included within the meaning of the term for purposes of the Convention. This expanded definition conforms to that in the OECD Model. The definition of "real property" ("immovable property") for purposes of Article 6 is more limited than the expansive definition of "real property situated in the Other Contracting State" in paragraph 2 of Article 13 (Gains). The Article 13 term includes not only immovable property as defined in Article 6 but certain other interests in real property.

Paragraph 3

Paragraph 3 makes clear that all forms of income derived from the exploitation of real property are taxable in the Contracting State in which the property is situated. In the case of a net lease of real property, if a net taxation election has not been made, the gross rental payment (before deductible expenses incurred by the lessee) is treated as income from the property. Income from the disposition of an interest in real property, however, is not considered "derived" from real property and is not dealt with in this article. The taxation of that income is addressed in Article 13 (Gains). Also, the interest paid on a mortgage on real property and distributions by a U.S. Real Estate Investment Trust are not dealt with in Article 6. Such payments would fall under Articles 10 (Dividends), 11 (Interest) or 13 (Gains). Finally, dividends paid by a United States Real Property Holding Corporation are not considered to be income from the exploitation of real property: such payments would fall under Article 10 (Dividends) or 13 (Gains).

Paragraph 4

This paragraph specifies that the basic rule of paragraph 1 (as elaborated in paragraph 3) applies to income from real property of an enterprise and to income from real property used for the performance of independent personal services. This clarifies that the situs country may tax the real property income (including rental income) of a resident of the other Contracting State in the absence of attribution to a permanent establishment or fixed base in the situs State. This provision represents an exception to the general rule under Articles 7 (Business Profits) and 14 (Independent Personal Services) that income must be attributable to a permanent establishment or fixed base, respectively, in order to be taxable in the situs state.

Paragraph 5

Paragraph 5 provides that a resident of one Contracting State that derives real property income from the other may elect, for any taxable year, to be subject to tax in that other State on a net basis, as though the income were attributable to a permanent establishment in that other State. The election may be terminated with the consent of the competent authority of the situs State. In the United States, revocation will be granted in accordance with the provisions of Treas. Reg. section 1.871-10(d)(2).

ARTICLE 7 (BUSINESS PROFITS)

This Article provides rules for the taxation by a Contracting State of the business profits of an enterprise of the other Contracting State.

Paragraph 1

Paragraph 1 states the general rule that business profits (as defined in paragraph 7) of an enterprise of one Contracting State may not be taxed by the other Contracting State unless the enterprise carries on business in that other Contracting State through a permanent establishment (as defined in Article 5 (Permanent Establishment)) situated there. When that condition is met, the State in which the permanent establishment is situated may tax the enterprise, on the income that is attributable to the permanent establishment, but only on a net basis.

Paragraph 2

Paragraph 2 provides rules for the attribution of business profits to a permanent establishment. The Contracting States will attribute to a permanent establishment the profits that it would have earned had it been an independent enterprise engaged in the same or similar activities under the same or similar circumstances. This language incorporates the arm's-length standard for purposes of determining the profits attributable to a permanent establishment. The computation of business profits attributable to a permanent establishment under this paragraph is subject to the rules of paragraph 3 for the allowance of expenses incurred for the purposes of earning the profits.

The "attributable to" concept of paragraph 2 is analogous but not entirely equivalent to the "effectively connected" concept in Code section 864(c). The profits attributable to a permanent establishment may be from sources within or without a Contracting State.

This Article does not contain a provision corresponding to paragraph 4 of Article 7 of the OECD Model. That paragraph provides that a Contracting State in certain circumstances may determine the profits attributable to a permanent establishment on the basis of an apportionment of the total profits of the enterprise. Any such approach, however, must be designed to approximate an arm's length result. The inclusion of such a paragraph is unnecessary. The U.S.

view is that paragraphs 2 and 3 of Article 7 authorize the use of such approaches independently of paragraph 4 of Article 7 of the OECD Model because total profits methods are acceptable methods for determining the arm's length profits of associated enterprises under Article 9 (Associated Enterprises). Accordingly, it is understood that, under paragraph 2 of the Convention, it is permissible to use methods other than separate accounting to determine the arm's length profits of a permanent establishment where it is necessary to do so for practical reasons, such as when the affairs of the permanent establishment are so closely bound up with those of the head office that it would be impossible to disentangle them on any strict basis of accounts.

Paragraph 3

This paragraph is in substance the same as paragraph 3 of Article 7 of the OECD Model, although it is in some respects more detailed. Paragraph 3 provides that in determining the business profits of a permanent establishment, deductions shall be allowed for the expenses incurred for the purposes of the permanent establishment, ensuring that business profits will be taxed on a net basis. This rule is not limited to expenses incurred exclusively for the purposes of the permanent establishment, but includes a reasonable allocation of expenses incurred for the purposes of the enterprise as a whole, or that part of the enterprise that includes the permanent establishment. Deductions are to be allowed regardless of which accounting unit of the enterprise books the expenses, so long as they are incurred for the purposes of the permanent establishment. For example, a portion of the interest expense recorded on the books of the home office in one State may be deducted by a permanent establishment in the other if properly allocable thereto.

The paragraph specifies that the expenses that may be considered to be incurred for the purposes of the permanent establishment are expenses for research and development, interest and other similar expenses, as well as a reasonable amount of executive and general administrative expenses. This rule permits (but does not require) each Contracting State to apply the type of expense allocation rules provided by U.S. law (such as in Treas. Reg. sections 1.861-8 and 1.882-5).

Paragraph 3 does not permit a deduction for expenses charged to a permanent establishment by another unit of the enterprise. Thus, a permanent establishment may not deduct a royalty deemed paid to the head office. Similarly, a permanent establishment may not increase its business profits by the amount of any notional fees for ancillary services performed for another unit of the enterprise, but also should not receive a deduction for the expense of providing such services, since those expenses would be incurred for purposes of a business unit other than the permanent establishment.

Paragraph 4

Paragraph 4 provides that no business profits can be attributed to a permanent establishment merely because it purchases goods or merchandise for the enterprise of which it is a part. This paragraph is essentially identical to paragraph 5 of Article 7 of the OECD Model. This rule applies only to an office that performs functions for the enterprise in addition to purchasing. The income attribution issue does not arise if the sole activity of the permanent establishment is the purchase of goods or merchandise because such activity does not give rise to a permanent establishment under Article 5 (Permanent Establishment). A common situation in which paragraph 4 is relevant is one in which a permanent establishment purchases raw materials for the enterprise's manufacturing operation conducted outside the United States and sells the manufactured product. While business profits may be attributable to the permanent establishment with respect to its sales activities, no profits are attributable to it with respect to its purchasing activities.

Paragraph 5

This paragraph essentially tracks paragraph 6 of Article 7 of the OECD Model, providing that profits shall be determined by the same method each year, unless there is good reason to change the method used. This rule assures consistent tax treatment over time for permanent establishments. It limits the ability of both the Contracting State and the enterprise to change accounting methods to be applied to the permanent establishment. It does not, however, restrict a Contracting State from imposing additional requirements, such as the rules under Code section 481, to prevent amounts from being duplicated or omitted following a change in accounting method.

Paragraph 5 also provides that the business profits attributed to a permanent establishment include only those profits derived from that permanent establishment's assets or activities, a rule found in Paragraph 2 of the U.S. Model. This rule is consistent with the "asset-use" and "business activities" test of Code section 864(c)(2). Thus, the limited force of attraction rule of Code section 864(c)(3) is not incorporated into paragraph 5.

Paragraph 6

Paragraph 6 coordinates the provisions of Article 7 and other provisions of the Convention. Under this paragraph, when business profits include items of income that are dealt with separately under other articles of the Convention, the provisions of those articles will, except when they specifically provide to the contrary, take precedence over the provisions of Article 7. For example, the taxation of dividends will be determined by the rules of Article 10 (Dividends), and not by Article 7, except where, as provided in paragraph 6 of Article 10, the dividend is attributable to a permanent establishment or fixed base. In the latter case the provisions of Articles 7 or 14 (Independent Personal Services) apply. Thus, an enterprise of one State deriving dividends from the other State may not rely on Article 7 to exempt those dividends from tax at source if they are not attributable to a permanent establishment of the enterprise in the other State. By the same token, if the dividends are attributable to a permanent establishment in the other State, the dividends may be taxed on a net income basis at the source State full corporate tax rate, rather than on a gross basis under Article 10 (Dividends).

As provided in Article 8 (Shipping and Air Transport), income derived from shipping and air transport activities in international traffic described in that Article is taxable only in the country of residence of the enterprise regardless of whether it is attributable to a permanent establishment situated in the source State.

Paragraph 7

The term "business profits" is defined broadly in paragraph 7 to mean income derived from any trade or business. Business profits includes income earned by an enterprise from the furnishing of personal services is business profits. Thus, a consulting firm resident in one State whose employees perform services in the other State through a permanent establishment may be taxed in that other State on a net basis under Article 7, and not under Article 14 (Independent Personal Services), which applies only to individuals or groups of individuals. The salaries of the employees would be subject to the rules of Article 15 (Dependent Personal Services).

In accordance with this broad definition, the term "business profits" includes income attributable to notional principal contracts and other financial instruments to the extent that the income is attributable to a trade or business of dealing in such instruments, or is otherwise related to a trade or business (as in the case of a notional principal contract entered into for the purpose of hedging currency risk arising from an active trade or business). Any other income derived from such instruments is, unless specifically covered in another article, dealt with under Article 21 (Other Income).

Paragraph 7 also specifies that the term "business profits" includes income derived by an enterprise from the rental of tangible personal property (movable property). The inclusion of income derived by an enterprise from the rental of tangible personal property in business profits means that such income earned by a resident of a Contracting State can be taxed by the other Contracting State only if the income is attributable to a permanent establishment maintained by the resident in that other State, and, if the income is taxable, it can be taxed only on a net basis. Income from the rental of tangible personal property that is not derived in connection with a trade or business is dealt with in Article 21 (Other Income).

Paragraph 8

Paragraph 8 incorporates into the Convention the rule of Code section 864(c)(6). Like the Code section on which it is based, paragraph 8 provides that any income or gain attributable to a permanent establishment or a fixed base during its existence is taxable in the Contracting State where the permanent establishment or fixed base is situated, even if the payment of that income or gain is deferred until after the permanent establishment or fixed base ceases to exist. This rule applies with respect to paragraphs 1 and 2 of Article 7 (Business Profits), paragraph 6 of Article 10 (Dividends), paragraph 5 of Articles 11 (Interest), Paragraph 4 of Article 12 (Royalties), Paragraph 3 of Article 13 (Gains), Article 14 (Independent Personal Services) and paragraph 2 of Article 21 (Other Income).

The effect of this rule can be illustrated by the following example. Assume a company that is a resident of Slovenia and that maintains a permanent establishment in the United States winds up the permanent establishment's business and sells the permanent establishment's inventory and assets to a U.S. buyer at the end of year 1 in exchange for an interest-bearing installment obligation payable in full at the end of year 3. Despite the fact that Article 13's threshold requirement for U.S. taxation is not met in year 3 because the company has no permanent establishment in the United States, the United States may tax the deferred income payment recognized by the company in year 3.

Relation to Other Articles

This Article is subject to the saving clause of paragraph 4 of Article 1 (General Scope) of the Convention. Thus, if a citizen of the United States who is a resident of Slovenia under the treaty derives business profits from the United States that are not attributable to a permanent establishment in the United States, the United States may, subject to the special foreign tax credit rules of paragraph 3 of Article 23 (Relief from Double Taxation), tax those profits, notwithstanding the provision of paragraph 1 of this Article which would exempt the income from U.S. tax.

The benefits of this Article are also subject to Article 22 (Limitation on Benefits). Thus, an enterprise of the Slovenia that derives income effectively connected with a U.S. trade or business may not claim the benefits of Article 7 unless the resident carrying on the enterprise qualifies for such benefits under Article 22.

ARTICLE 8 (SHIPPING AND AIR TRANSPORT)

This Article governs the taxation of profits from the operation of ships and aircraft in international traffic. The term "international traffic" is defined in subparagraph 1(d) of Article 3 (General Definitions). The taxation of gains from the alienation of ships, aircraft or containers is not dealt with in this Article but in paragraph 4 of Article 13 (Gains).

Paragraph 1

Paragraph 1 provides that profits derived by an enterprise of a Contracting State from the operation in international traffic of ships or aircraft are taxable only in that Contracting State. Because paragraph 6 of Article 7 (Business Profits) defers to Article 8 with respect to shipping income, such income derived by a resident of one of the Contracting States may not be taxed in the other State even if the enterprise has a permanent establishment in that other State. Thus, if a U.S. airline has a ticket office in Slovenia, Slovenia may not tax the airline's profits attributable to that office under Article 7. Since entities engaged in international transportation activities normally will have many permanent establishments in a number of countries, the rule avoids difficulties that would be encountered in attributing income to multiple permanent establishments if the income were covered by Article 7 (Business Profits).

Paragraph 2

The income from the operation of ships or aircraft in international traffic that is exempt from tax under paragraph 1 is defined in paragraph 2. In addition to income derived directly from the operation of ships and aircraft in international traffic, this definition also includes certain items of rental income that are closely related to those activities. First, income of an enterprise of a Contracting State from the rental of ships or aircraft on a full basis (i.e., with crew) when such ships or aircraft are used in international traffic is income of the lessor from the operation of ships and aircraft in international traffic and, therefore, is exempt from tax in the other Contracting State under paragraph 1. Also, paragraph 2 encompasses income from the lease of ships or aircraft on a bareboat basis (i.e., without crew), either when the ships or aircraft are operated in international traffic by the lessee, or when the income is incidental to other income of the lessor from the operation of ships or aircraft in international traffic. The scope of Article 8 is thus the same as the U.S. Model, but broader than that of the OECD Model as it covers rentals from bareboat leasing that are not incidental to the operation of ships or aircraft by the resident itself.

Paragraph 2 also clarifies, consistent with the Commentary to Article 8 of the OECD Model, that income earned by an enterprise from the inland transport of property or passengers within either Contracting State falls within Article 8 if the transport is undertaken as part of the international transport of property or passengers by the enterprise. Thus, if a U.S. shipping company contracts to carry property from Slovenia to a U.S. city and, as part of that contract, it transports the property by truck from its point of origin to an airport in Slovenia (or it contracts with a trucking company to carry the property to the airport) the income earned by the U.S. shipping company from the overland leg of the journey would be taxable only in the United States. Similarly, Article 8 also would apply to income from lighterage undertaken as part of the international transport of goods.

Finally, certain non-transport activities that are an integral part of the services performed by a transport company are understood to be covered in paragraph 1, though they are not specified in paragraph 2. These include, for example, the performance of some maintenance or catering services by one airline for another airline, if these services are incidental to the provision of those services by the airline for itself. Income earned by concessionaires, however, is not covered by Article 8. These interpretations of paragraph 1 also are consistent with the Commentary to Article 8 of the OECD Model.

Paragraph 3

Under this paragraph, profits of an enterprise of a Contracting State from the use, maintenance or rental of containers (including equipment for their transport) that are used for the transport of goods in international traffic are exempt from tax in the other Contracting State. This result obtains under paragraph 3 regardless of whether the recipient of the income is engaged in the operation of ships or aircraft in international traffic, and regardless of whether the enterprise has a permanent establishment in the other Contracting State. By contrast, Article 8 of the OECD

Model covers only income from the use, maintenance or rental of containers that is incidental to other income from international traffic.

Paragraph 4

This paragraph clarifies that the provisions of paragraphs 1 and 3 also apply to profits derived by an enterprise of a Contracting State from participation in a pool, joint business or international operating agency. This refers to various arrangements for international cooperation by carriers in shipping and air transport. For example, airlines from two countries may agree to share the transport of passengers between the two countries. They each will fly the same number of flights per week and share the revenues from that route equally, regardless of the number of passengers that each airline actually transports. Paragraph 4 makes clear that with respect to each carrier the income dealt with in the Article is that carrier's share of the total transport, not the income derived from the passengers actually carried by the airline. This paragraph corresponds to paragraph 4 of Article 8 of the OECD Model.

Relation to Other Articles

As with other benefits of the Convention, the benefit of exclusive residence country taxation under Article 8 is available to an enterprise only if it is entitled to benefits under Article 22 (Limitation on Benefits).

This Article also is subject to the saving clause of paragraph 4 of Article 1 (General Scope) of the Convention. Thus, if a citizen of the United States who is a resident of Slovenia derives profits from the operation of ships or aircraft in international traffic, notwithstanding the exclusive residence country taxation in paragraph 1 of Article 8, the United States may, subject to the special foreign tax credit rules of paragraph 3 of Article 23 (Relief from Double Taxation), tax those profits as part of the worldwide income of the citizen. (This is an unlikely situation, however, because non-tax considerations (e.g., insurance) generally result in shipping activities being carried on in corporate form.)

ARTICLE 9 (ASSOCIATED ENTERPRISES)

This Article incorporates in the Convention the arm's-length principle reflected in the U.S. domestic transfer pricing provisions, particularly Code section 482. It provides that when related enterprises engage in a transaction on terms that are not arm's-length, the Contracting States may make appropriate adjustments to the taxable income and tax liability of such related enterprises to reflect what the income and tax of these enterprises with respect to the transaction would have been had there been an arm's-length relationship between them.

Paragraph 1

This paragraph addresses the situation where an enterprise of a Contracting State is related to an enterprise of the other Contracting State, and there are arrangements or conditions imposed between the enterprises in their commercial or financial relations that are different from those that would have existed in the absence of the relationship. Under these circumstances, the Contracting States may adjust the income (or loss) of the enterprise to reflect what it would have been in the absence of such a relationship.

The paragraph identifies the relationships between enterprises that serve as a prerequisite to application of the Article. As the Commentary to the OECD Model makes clear, the necessary element in these relationships is effective control, which is also the standard for purposes of section 482. Thus, the Article applies if an enterprise of one State participates directly or indirectly in the management, control, or capital of the enterprise of the other State. Also, the Article applies if any third person or persons participate directly or indirectly in the management, control, or capital of enterprises of different States. For this purpose, all types of control are included, i.e., whether or not legally enforceable and however exercised or exercisable.

The fact that a transaction is entered into between such related enterprises does not, in and of itself, mean that a Contracting State may adjust the income (or loss) of one or both of the enterprises under the provisions of this Article. If the conditions of the transaction are consistent with those that would be made between independent persons, the income arising from that trans-action should not be subject to adjustment under this Article.

Similarly, the fact that associated enterprises may have concluded arrangements, such as cost sharing arrangements or general services agreements, is not in itself an indication that the two enterprises have entered into a non-arm's-length transaction that should give rise to an adjustment under paragraph 1. Both related and unrelated parties enter into such arrangements (e.g., joint venturers may share some development costs). As with any other kind of transaction, when related parties enter into an arrangement, the specific arrangement must be examined to see whether or not it meets the arm's-length standard. In the event that it does not, an appropriate adjustment may be made, which may include modifying the terms of the agreement or recharacterizing the transaction to reflect its substance.

It is understood that the "commensurate with income" standard for determining appropriate transfer prices for intangibles, added to Code section 482 by the Tax Reform Act of 1986, was designed to operate consistently with the arm's-length standard. The implementation of this standard in the section 482 regulations is in accordance with the general principles of paragraph 1 of Article 9 of the Convention, as interpreted by the OECD Transfer Pricing Guidelines.

It also is understood that the Contracting States preserve their rights to apply internal law provisions relating to adjustments between related parties. They also reserve the right to make adjustments in cases involving tax evasion or fraud. Such adjustments -- the distribution, appor-tionment, or allocation of income, deductions, credits or allowances -- are permitted even if they are different from, or go beyond, those authorized by paragraph 1 of the Article, as long as they accord with the general principles of paragraph 1, i.e., that the adjustment reflects what would have transpired had the related parties been acting at arm's length. For example, while paragraph 1 explicitly allows adjustments of deductions in computing taxable income, it does not deal with adjustments to tax credits. It does not, however, preclude such adjustments if they can be made under internal law. The OECD Model reaches the same result. See paragraph 4 of the Commentaries to Article 9.

This Article also permits tax authorities to deal with thin capitalization issues. They may, in the context of Article 9, scrutinize more than the rate of interest charged on a loan between related persons. They also may examine the capital structure of an enterprise, whether a payment in respect of that loan should be treated as interest, and, if it is treated as interest, under what circumstances interest deductions should be allowed to the payor. Paragraph 2 of the Commentaries to Article 9 of the OECD Model, together with the U.S. observation set forth in paragraph 15 thereof, sets forth a similar understanding of the scope of Article 9 in the context of thin capitalization.

Paragraph 2

When a Contracting State has made an adjustment that is consistent with the provisions of paragraph 1, and the other Contracting State agrees that the adjustment was appropriate to reflect arm's-length conditions, that other Contracting State is obligated to make a correlative adjustment (sometimes referred to as a "corresponding adjustment") to the tax liability of the related person in that other Contracting State. Although the OECD Model does not specify that the other Contracting State must agree with the initial adjustment before it is obligated to make the correlative adjustment, the Commentary makes clear that the paragraph is to be read that way.

As explained in the OECD Commentaries, Article 9 leaves the treatment of "secondary adjustments" to the laws of the Contracting States. When an adjustment under Article 9 has been made, one of the parties will have in its possession funds that it would not have had at arm's length. The question arises as to how to treat these funds. In the United States the general practice is to treat such funds as a dividend or contribution to capital, depending on the relationship between the parties. Under certain circumstances, the parties may be permitted to restore the funds to the party that would have the funds at arm's length, and to establish an account payable pending restoration of the funds. See Rev. Proc. 99-32, 1999-34 I.R.B. 296.

The Contracting State making a secondary adjustment will take the other provisions of the Convention, where relevant, into account. For example, if the effect of a secondary adjustment is to treat a U.S. corporation as having made a distribution of profits to its parent corporation in Slovenia, the provisions of Article 10 (Dividends) will apply, and the United States may impose a 5 percent withholding tax on the dividend. Also, if under Article 23, Slovenia generally gives a credit for taxes paid with respect to such dividends, it would also be required to do so in this case.

The competent authorities are authorized by paragraph 2 to consult, if necessary, to resolve any differences in the application of these provisions. For example, there may be a disagreement over whether an adjustment made by a Contracting State under paragraph 1 was appropriate.

If a correlative adjustment is made under paragraph 2, it is to be implemented, pursuant to paragraph 2 of Article 25 (Mutual Agreement Procedure), notwithstanding any time limits or other procedural limitations in the law of the Contracting State making the adjustment. If a taxpayer has entered a closing agreement (or other written settlement) with the United States prior to bringing a case to the competent authorities, the U.S. competent authority will endeavor only to obtain a correlative adjustment from Slovenia. See, Rev. Proc. 96-13, 1996-13 I.R.B. 31, Section 7.05.

Relationship to Other Articles

The saving clause of paragraph 4 of Article 1 (General Scope) does not apply to paragraph 2 of Article 9 by virtue of the exceptions to the saving clause in paragraph 5(a) of Article 1. Thus, even if the statute of limitations has run, a refund of tax can be made in order to implement a correlative adjustment. Statutory or procedural limitations, however, cannot be overridden to impose additional tax, because paragraph 2 of Article 1 provides that the Convention cannot restrict any statutory benefit.

ARTICLE 10 (DIVIDENDS)

Article 10 provides rules for the taxation of dividends paid by a resident of one Contracting State to a beneficial owner that is a resident of the other Contracting State. The article provides for full residence country taxation of such dividends and a limited source-State right to tax. Article 10 also provides rules for the imposition of a tax on branch profits by the State of source. Finally, the article prohibits a State from imposing a tax on dividends paid by companies resident in the other Contracting State and from imposing taxes, other than a branch profits tax, on undistributed earnings.

Paragraph 1

The right of a shareholder's country of residence to tax dividends arising in the source country is preserved by paragraph 1, which permits a Contracting State to tax its residents on dividends paid to them by a resident of the other Contracting State. For dividends from any other source paid to a resident, Article 21 (Other Income) grants the residence country exclusive taxing jurisdiction (other than for dividends attributable to a permanent establishment or fixed base in the other State).

Paragraph 2

The State of source may also tax dividends beneficially owned by a resident of the other State, subject to the limitations in paragraph 2. Generally, the source State's tax is limited to 15 percent of the gross amount of the dividend paid. If, however, the beneficial owner of the dividends is a company resident in the other State that holds at least 25 percent of the voting stock (or in the case of Slovenia, if there is no voting stock, at least 25 percent of the statutory capital) of the company paying the dividend, then the source State's tax is limited to 5 percent of the gross amount of the dividend. Indirect ownership of voting shares (through tiers of corporations) and direct ownership of non-voting shares are not taken into account for purposes of determining eligibility for the 5 percent direct dividend rate. Shares are considered voting shares if they provide the power to elect, appoint or replace any person vested with the powers ordinarily exercised by the board of directors of a U.S. corporation.

The benefits of paragraph 2 may be granted at the time of payment by means of reduced withholding at source. It also is consistent with the paragraph for tax to be withheld at the time of payment at full statutory rates, and the treaty benefit to be granted by means of a subsequent refund so long as such procedures are applied in a reasonable manner.

Paragraph 2 does not affect the taxation of the profits out of which the dividends are paid. The taxation by a Contracting State of the income of its resident companies is governed by the internal law of the Contracting State, subject to the provisions of paragraph 4 of Article 24 (Non-Discrimination).

The term "beneficial owner" is not defined in the Convention, and is, therefore, defined as under the internal law of the country imposing tax (i.e., the source country). The beneficial owner of the dividend for purposes of Article 10 is the person to which the dividend income is attributable for tax purposes under the laws of the source State. Thus, if a dividend paid by a corporation that is a resident of one of the States (as determined under Article 4 (Residence)) is received by a nominee or agent that is a resident of the other State on behalf of a person that is not a resident of that other State, the dividend is not entitled to the benefits of this Article. However, a dividend received by a nominee on behalf of a resident of that other State would be entitled to benefits. These limitations are confirmed by paragraph 12 of the OECD Commentaries to Article 10. See also, paragraph 24 of the OECD Commentaries to Article 1 (General Scope).

Companies holding shares through fiscally transparent entities such as partnerships are considered for purposes of this paragraph to hold their proportionate interest in the shares held by the intermediate entity. As a result, companies holding shares through such entities may be able to claim the benefits of subparagraph (a) under certain circumstances. The lower rate applies when the company's proportionate share of the shares held by the intermediate entity meets the 25 percent voting stock threshold. Whether this ownership threshold is satisfied may be difficult to determine and often will require an analysis of the partnership or trust agreement.

Paragraph 3

Paragraph 3 provides rules that modify the maximum rates of tax at source provided in paragraph 2 in particular cases. The first sentence of paragraph 3 denies the lower direct investment withholding rate of paragraph 2(a) for dividends paid by a U.S. Regulated Investment Company (RIC) or a U.S. Real Estate Investment Trust (REIT). The second sentence states that dividends paid by a RIC will qualify for the 15 percent rate provided by subparagraph 2(b).

The third sentence denies the benefits of both subparagraphs (a) and (b) of paragraph 2 to dividends paid by REITs in certain circumstances, allowing them to be taxed at the U.S. statutory rate (30 percent). The United States limits the source tax on dividends paid by a REIT to the 15 percent rate only when the beneficial owner of the dividend satisfies one or more of three criteria. First, the dividend may qualify if the beneficial owner is an individual resident of the other State who owns not more than 10 percent of the REIT. Second, the dividend may qualify for the 15 percent rate if it is paid with respect to a class of stock that is publicly traded and the beneficial owner of the dividends is a person holding an interest of not more than 5 percent of any class of the REIT's stock. Finally, the dividend may qualify for the 15 percent rate if the beneficial owner of the dividend is a person holding an interest of not more than 10 percent of the REIT and the REIT is diversified.

For this purpose, a REIT will be considered diversified if the value of no single interest in the REIT's real property exceeds 10 percent of the REIT's total interests in real property. For purposes of this rule, foreclosure property and mortgages will not be considered an interest in real property unless, in the case of a mortgage, it has substantial equity components. With respect to partnership interests held by a REIT, the REIT will be treated as owning directly the interests in real property held by the partnership.

The denial of the 5 percent withholding rate at source to all RIC and REIT shareholders, and the denial of the 15 percent rate to REIT shareholders that do not meet one of the 3 tests described above, is intended to prevent the use of these entities to gain unjustifiable source taxation benefits for certain shareholders resident in Slovenia. For example, a corporation resident in Slovenia that wishes to hold a diversified portfolio of U.S. corporate shares may hold the portfolio directly and pay a U.S. withholding tax of 15 percent on all of the dividends that it receives. Alternatively, it may acquire a diversified portfolio by purchasing a 25 percent or more of the interests in a RIC. Since the RIC may be a pure conduit, there may be no U.S. tax costs to interposing the RIC in the chain of ownership. Absent the special rule in paragraph 3, such use of the RIC could transform portfolio dividends, taxable in the United States under the Convention at 15 percent, into direct investment dividends taxable only at 5 percent.

Similarly, a resident of Slovenia directly holding U.S. real property would pay U.S. tax either at a 30 percent rate on the gross income or at graduated rates on the net income. As in the preceding example, by placing the real property in a REIT, the investor could transform real estate income into dividend income, taxable at the rates provided in Article 10, significantly reducing the U.S. tax that otherwise would be imposed. This policy avoids a disparity between the taxation of direct real estate investments and real estate investments made through REIT conduits. In the cases covered by the exceptions, the holding in the REIT is not considered the equivalent of a direct holding in the underlying real property.

Paragraph 4

Paragraph 4 exempts from tax in the state of source, dividends paid to qualified governmental entities. Although there is no analogous provision in the OECD Model, the exemption of paragraph 4 is analogous to that provided to foreign governments under section 892 of the Code. Paragraph 4 makes that exemption reciprocal. A qualified governmental entity is defined in paragraph 1(i) of Article 3 (General Definitions), and it includes a government pension plan. The definition does not include a governmental entity that carries on commercial activity. Further, a dividend paid by a company engaged in commercial activity that is controlled (within the meaning of Treas. Reg. section 1.892-5T) by a qualified governmental entity that is the beneficial owner of the dividend is not exempt at source under paragraph 4 because ownership of a controlled company is viewed as a substitute for carrying on a business directly.

Paragraph 5

Paragraph 5 defines the term dividends broadly and flexibly. The definition is intended to cover all arrangements that yield a return on an equity investment in a corporation as determined under the tax law of the state of source, as well as arrangements that might be developed in the future.

The term dividends includes income from shares, or other corporate rights that are not treated as debt under the law of the source State, that participate in the profits of the company. The term also includes income that is subjected to the same tax treatment as income from shares by the law of the State of source. Thus, a constructive dividend that results from a non-arm's length transaction between a corporation and a related party is a dividend. In the case of the United States, the term dividend includes amounts treated as a dividend under U.S. law upon the sale or redemption of shares or upon a transfer of shares in a reorganization. See, e.g., Rev. Rul. 92-85, 1992-2 C.B. 69 (sale of foreign subsidiary's stock to U.S. sister company is a deemed dividend to extent of subsidiary's and sister's earnings and profits). Further, a distribution from a U.S. publicly traded limited partnership, which is taxed as a corporation under U.S. law, is a dividend for purposes of Article 10. However, a distribution by a limited liability company is not characterized by the United States as a dividend and, therefore, is not a dividend for purposes of Article 10, provided the limited liability company is not characterized as an association taxable as a corporation under U.S. law. Finally, a payment denominated as interest that is made by a thinly capitalized corporation may be treated as a dividend to the extent that the debt is recharacterized as equity under the laws of the source State.

Paragraph 6

Paragraph 6 excludes from the general source country limitations under paragraph 2 dividends paid with respect to holdings that form part of the business property of a permanent establishment or a fixed base. Such dividends will be taxed on a net basis using the rates and rules of taxation generally applicable to residents of the State in which the permanent establishment or fixed base is located, as modified by the Convention. An example of dividends paid with respect to the business property of a permanent establishment would be dividends derived by a dealer in stock or securities from stock or securities that the dealer held for sale to customers.

In the case of a permanent establishment or fixed base that once existed in the State but that no longer exists, the provisions of paragraph 6 also apply, by virtue of paragraph 8 of Article 7 (Business Profits), to dividends that would be attributable to such a permanent establishment or fixed base if it did exist in the year of payment or accrual. See the Technical Explanation of paragraph 8 of Article 7.

Paragraph 7

A State's right to tax dividends paid by a company that is a resident of the other State is restricted by paragraph 7 to cases in which the dividends are paid to a resident of that State or are attributable to a permanent establishment or fixed base in that State. Thus, a State may not impose a "secondary" withholding tax on dividends paid by a nonresident company out of earnings and profits from that State. In the case of the United States, paragraph 7, therefore, overrides the ability to impose taxes under sections 871 and 882(a) on dividends paid by foreign corporations that have a U.S. source under section 861(a)(2)(B).

The paragraph also restricts a State's right to impose corporate level taxes on undistributed profits, other than a branch profits tax. The accumulated earnings tax and the personal holding company taxes are taxes covered in Article 2 (Taxes Covered). Accordingly, under the provisions of Article 7 (Business Profits), the United States may not impose those taxes on the income of a resident of the other State except to the extent that income is attributable to a permanent establishment in the United States. Paragraph 7 also confirms the denial of the U.S. authority to impose those taxes. The paragraph does not restrict a State's right to tax its resident shareholders on undistributed earnings of a corporation resident in the other State. Thus, the U.S. authority to impose the foreign personal holding company tax, its taxes on subpart F income and on an increase in earnings invested in U.S. property, and its tax on income of a passive foreign investment company that is a qualified electing fund is in no way restricted by this provision.

Paragraph 8

Paragraph 8 permits a State to impose a branch profits tax on a corporation resident in the other State. The tax is in addition to other taxes permitted by the Convention. Since the term "corporation" is not defined in the Convention, it will be defined for this purpose under the law of the first-mentioned (i.e., source) State.

A State may impose a branch profits tax on a corporation if the corporation has income attributable to a permanent establishment in that State, derives income from real property in that State that is taxed on a net basis under Article 6 (Income from Real Property (Immovable Property)), or realizes gains taxable in that State under paragraph 1 of Article 13 (Gains). The tax is limited, however, to the aforementioned items of income that are included in the "dividend equivalent amount."

Paragraph 8 permits the United States generally to impose its branch profits tax on a corporation resident in Slovenia to the extent of the corporation's (i) business profits that are attributable to a permanent establishment in the United States, (ii) income that is subject to taxation on a net basis because the corporation has elected under section 882(d) of the Code to treat income from real property not otherwise taxed on a net basis as effectively connected income, and (iii) gain from the disposition of a United States Real Property Interest, other than an interest in a United States Real Property Holding Corporation. The United States may not impose its branch profits tax on the business profits of a corporation resident in Slovenia that are effectively connected with a U.S. trade or business but that are not attributable to a permanent establishment and are not otherwise subject to U.S. taxation under Article 6 (Income from Real Property (Immovable Property)) or paragraph 1 of Article 13 (Gains).

The term "dividend equivalent amount" used in paragraph 8 has the same meaning that it has under section 884 of the Code, as amended from time to time, provided the amendments are consistent with the purpose of the branch profits tax. Generally, the dividend equivalent amount for a particular year is the income described above that is included in the corporation's effectively connected earnings and profits for that year, after payment of the corporate tax under Articles 6 (Income from Real Property (Immovable Property)), 7 (Business Profits) or 13 (Gains), reduced for any increase in the branch's U.S. net equity during the year or increased for any reduction in its U.S. net equity during the year. U.S. net equity is U.S. assets less U.S. liabilities. See Treas. Reg. section 1.884-1. The dividend equivalent amount for any year approximates the dividend that a U.S. branch office would have paid during the year if the branch had been operated as a separate U.S. subsidiary company. In the case that Slovenia also enacts a branch profits tax, the base of its tax is limited to an amount that is analogous to the dividend equivalent amount.

Paragraph 9

Paragraph 9 provides that the branch profits tax permitted by paragraph 8 shall not be imposed at a rate exceeding the direct investment dividend withholding rate of five percent.

Paragraph 10

Paragraph 10 provides that the benefits of this Article will be denied in cases in which the main purpose, or one of the main purposes, for the creation or assignment of shares or other rights in respect of which dividends are paid is to take advantage of this Article.

This provision addresses abusive transactions that would not be caught by the provisions of Article 22 (Limitation on Benefits) because the purported recipient of the income qualifies under that Article. For example, an abuse that would not be caught by the Limitation on Benefits provisions involves "dividend washing". A bank that is a resident of Slovenia and that easily can meet any of the tests under a limitation on benefits provision may decide to "sell" its treaty qualification to a customer that does not so qualify because it is a resident of a third country. One way that it could do so would be for the bank to purchase shares in a U.S. company that are owned by the customer immediately before the record date for dividends to be paid on the shares. At the same time, the bank would enter into a "repurchase" agreement under which it agreed with the customer to "resell" the shares to the customer on a certain date at a certain price. The main purpose of the agreement would be to qualify for reduced withholding tax under the Convention, without the bank incurring any actual market risk.

Similarly, taxpayers that qualify for Convention benefits could enter into transactions that are intended to increase the benefits that they otherwise would receive under the Convention. For example, under the Convention, if the beneficial owner of a dividend is a company that holds at least 25 percent of the voting stock of the company paying the dividend, the source-country rate is limited to 5 percent, rather than 15 percent. A company resident in Slovenia with an ownership interest of less than 25 percent in a U.S. company could enter into a transaction to increase temporarily its holding of stock to 25 percent mainly for the purpose of securing the reduced dividend withholding rate under the Convention. Because the Slovenian company would qualify for benefits under Article 22 (Limitation on Benefits), that Article would not address this transaction.

The Commentary to Article 1 of the OECD Model and the OECD Report on Harmful Tax Competition make clear that countries can impose their internal anti-abuse rules to deny claims for treaty benefits. The United States has a number of such rules and doctrines and they may reach the above cases. Because some have argued that these internal rules and doctrines do not apply in the above cases, paragraph 10 clarifies that anti-abuse rules can be applied to deny treaty benefits to transactions entered into with a main purpose of taking advantage of the Article. The provision has been added because of a proliferation of such schemes in recent years, but the lack of the provision in other treaties does not imply that internal anti-abuse rules do not apply. Although the provision uses the term "main purpose", which has gained international acceptance, it is intended to have the same meaning as the term "principal purpose", and the United States will interpret it that way.

The provision has gained international currency because other countries may not have as many domestic tools to prevent abuse as the United States. For them, the explicit inclusion of a main purpose standard in a treaty may be necessary to prevent abuses of the treaty. Even in the United States, taxpayers frequently have argued that a transaction qualifies for treaty benefits unless there is specific guidance to the contrary.

The provision is narrower, and provides a more definitive standard to taxpayers, than anti-abuse provisions that are included in certain bilateral treaties between other countries. In the broadest of those provisions, the competent authorities have unfettered discretion to deny the benefits of the treaty with respect to any transaction if, in their opinion, the receipt of those benefits, under the circumstances, would constitute an abuse of the Convention according to its purposes.

The provisions of paragraph 10 are self-executing and will apply even if guidance addressing a particular transaction has not yet been issued. Taxpayers therefore will be expected to determine whether one of the principal purposes of a particular transaction was to take advantage of the provision. The tax authorities of one of the Contracting States may, on review, however, deny the benefits of this Article. Moreover, the competent authorities of both Contracting States may together agree that this standard has been met in a particular case or with respect to a specific transaction entered into by a number of taxpayers. See Technical Explanation to paragraph 3 of Article 25 (Mutual Agreement Procedure). Such agreements, along with U.S. statutory, regulatory, and common law, will provide guidance to taxpayers regarding the scope of the provision.

Relation to Other Articles

Notwithstanding the foregoing limitations on source country taxation of dividends, the saving clause of paragraph 3 of Article 1 (General Scope) permits the United States to tax dividends received by its residents and citizens, subject to the special foreign tax credit rules of paragraph 3 of Article 23 (Relief from Double Taxation), as if the Convention had not come into effect.

The benefits of this Article are also subject to the provisions of Article 22 (Limitation on Benefits). Thus, if a resident of Slovenia is the beneficial owner of dividends paid by a U.S. corporation, the shareholder must qualify for treaty benefits under at least one of the tests of Article 22 in order to receive the benefits of this Article.

ARTICLE 11 (INTEREST)

Article 11 provides rules for the taxation of interest paid by a resident of one Contracting State to a beneficial owner that is a resident of the other Contracting State. The Article provides for full residence country taxation of such interest and a limited source country right to tax.

Paragraph 1

Paragraph 1 preserves the right of a Contracting State to tax interest paid to its residents that arises in the other Contracting State. For interest from any other source paid to a resident, Article 21 (Other Income) grants the residence country exclusive taxing jurisdiction (other than for interest attributable to a permanent establishment or fixed base in the other State).

Paragraph 2

Paragraph 2 grants to the source State the right to tax interest payments beneficially owned by a resident of the other Contracting State. The general rate of source country tax applicable to interest payments under paragraph 2 is limited to 5 percent. Under the provisions of paragraph 3 certain classes of interest payments are exempt from source country tax.

The term "beneficial owner" is not defined in the Convention, and is, therefore, defined as under the internal law of the country imposing tax (i.e., the source country). The beneficial owner of interest for purposes of Article 11 is the person to which the interest income is attributable for tax purposes under the laws of the source State. Thus, if interest arising in one of the States is received by a nominee or agent that is a resident of the other State on behalf of a person that is not a resident of that other State, the interest is not entitled to the benefits of this Article. However, interest received by a nominee on behalf of a resident of that other State would be entitled to benefits. These limitations are confirmed by paragraph 8 of the OECD Commentary on Article 11. See also, paragraph 24 of the OECD Commentaries to Article 1 (General Scope).

Paragraph 3

Paragraph 3 specifies certain categories of interest that are exempt from source State taxation. Subparagraph (a) exempts interest arising in one Contracting State and beneficially owned by a qualified governmental entity of the other Contracting State, as long as the qualified governmental entity does not control the person paying the interest. Subparagraph (b) exempts interest paid or accrued with respect to a debt obligation that is guaranteed or insured by a qualified governmental entity of the other Contracting State. Finally, subparagraph (c) exempts interest paid with respect to a deferred payment for personal property (movable property) or services.

Paragraph 4

The term "interest" as used in Article 11 is defined in paragraph 4 to include, inter alia, income from debt claims of every kind, whether or not secured by a mortgage. Penalty charges for late payment are excluded from the definition of interest. Interest that is paid or accrued subject to a contingency is within the ambit of Article 11. This includes income from a debt obligation carrying the right to participate in profits. The term does not, however, include amounts that are treated as dividends under Article 10 (Dividends).

The term interest also includes amounts subject to the same tax treatment as income from money lent under the law of the State in which the income arises. Thus, for purposes of the Convention, amounts that the United States will treat as interest include (i) the difference between the issue price and the stated redemption price at maturity of a debt instrument, i.e., original issue discount (OID), which may be wholly or partially realized on the disposition of a debt instrument (section 1273), (ii) amounts that are imputed interest on a deferred sales contract (section 483),

(iii) amounts treated as interest or OID under the stripped bond rules (section 1286), (iv) amounts treated as original issue discount under the below-market interest rate rules (section 7872), (v) a partner's distributive share of a partnership's interest income (section 702), (vi) the interest portion of periodic payments made under a "finance lease" or similar contractual arrangement that in substance is a borrowing by the nominal lessee to finance the acquisition of property, (vii) amounts included in the income of a holder of a residual interest in a REMIC (section 860E), because these amounts generally are subject to the same taxation treatment as interest under U.S. tax law, and (viii) embedded interest with respect to notional principal contracts.

Paragraph 5

Paragraph 5 provides an exception to the taxing rules of paragraphs 1, 2, and 3, in cases where the beneficial owner of the interest carries on business through a permanent establishment in the State of source or performs independent personal services from a fixed base situated in that State and the interest is attributable to that permanent establishment or fixed base. In such cases the provisions of Article 7 (Business Profits) or Article 14 (Independent Personal Services) will apply and the State of source will retain the right to impose tax on such interest income.

In the case of a permanent establishment or fixed base that once existed in the State but that no longer exists, the provisions of paragraph 5 also apply, by virtue of paragraph 8 of Article 7 (Business Profits), to interest that would be attributable to such a permanent establishment or fixed base if it did exist in the year of payment or accrual. See the Technical Explanation of paragraph 8 of Article 7.

Paragraph 6

Paragraph 6 provides rules for sourcing interest. Generally, interest is deemed to arise in a Contracting State when the payer is a resident of that State. When the payer of the interest has a permanent establishment or fixed base in a Contracting State and the interest is borne by the permanent establishment or fixed base, then the interest is deemed to arise in the State where the permanent establishment or fixed base is located. This rule applies whether or not the person paying the interest is a resident of a Contracting State. Thus, for example, if an enterprise of a third state had a permanent establishment in the United States, the United States could impose tax on interest paid by the permanent establishment to a resident of Slovenia, but only at the rates provided by paragraph 2 and 3.

Paragraph 7

Paragraph 7 provides that in cases involving special relationships between persons, Article 11 applies only to that portion of the total interest payments between those persons that would have been made absent such special relationships (i.e., an arm's-length interest payment). Any excess amount of interest paid remains taxable according to the laws of the United States and Slovenia, respectively, with due regard to the other provisions of the Convention. Thus, if the excess amount would be treated under the source country's law as a distribution of profits by a corporation, such amount could be taxed as a dividend rather than as interest, but the tax would be subject, if appropriate, to the rate limitations of paragraph 2 of Article 10 (Dividends).

The term "special relationship" is not defined in the Convention. In applying this paragraph the United States considers the term to include the relationships described in Article 9 (Associated Enterprises), which in turn correspond to the definition of "control" for purposes of section 482 of the Code.

This paragraph does not address cases where, owing to a special relationship between the payer and the beneficial owner or between both of them and some other person, the amount of the interest is less than an arm's-length amount. In those cases a transaction may be characterized to reflect its substance and interest may be imputed consistent with the definition of interest in paragraph 4. Consistent with Article 9 (Associated Enterprises), the United States would apply section 482 or 7872 of the Code to determine the amount of imputed interest in those cases.

Paragraph 8

Paragraph 8 provides anti-abuse exceptions to the source-country tax rules in paragraphs, 2 and 3, for two classes of interest payments.

The first exception, in subparagraph (a) of paragraph 8, deals with so-called "contingent interest." Under this provision interest arising in one of the Contracting States that is determined by reference to the receipts, sales, income, profits or other cash flow of the debtor or a related person, to any change in the value of any property of the debtor or a related person or to any dividend, partnership distribution or similar payment made by the debtor to a related person, also may be taxed in the Contracting State in which it arises, and according to the laws of that State, but if the beneficial owner is a resident of the other Contracting State, the gross amount of the interest may be taxed at a rate not exceeding the rate prescribed in subparagraph (b) of paragraph 2 of Article 10 (Dividends).

The second exception, in subparagraph (b) of paragraph 8, is consistent with the policy of Code sections 860E(e) and 860G(b) that excess inclusions with respect to a real estate mortgage investment conduit (REMIC) should bear full U.S. tax in all cases. Without a full tax at source foreign purchasers of residual interests would have a competitive advantage over U.S. purchasers at the time these interests are initially offered. Also, absent this rule the U.S. fisc would suffer a revenue loss with respect to mortgages held in a REMIC because of opportunities for tax avoidance created by differences in the timing of taxable and economic income produced by these interests.

Paragraph 9

Paragraph 9 extends the coverage of Article 11 to include the branch level interest tax on a corporation resident in Slovenia. The base of this tax is the excess, if any, of the interest deductible in the United States in computing the profits of the corporation that are subject to tax in the United States and either attributable to a permanent establishment in the United States or subject to tax in the United States under Article 6 (Income from Real Property (Immovable Property)) or Article 13 (Gains) of this Convention over the interest paid by or from the permanent establishment or trade or business in the United States.

Paragraph 10

Paragraph 10 provides that the benefits of this Article will be denied in cases in which the main purpose, or one of the main purposes, for the creation or assignment of the debt-claim in respect of which the interest is paid is to take advantage of this Article. This provision is analogous to paragraph 10 of Article 10 (Dividends), discussed above.

Relation to Other Articles

Notwithstanding the foregoing limitations on source country taxation of interest, the saving clause of paragraph 4 of Article 1 (General Scope) permits the United States to tax its residents and citizens, subject to the special foreign tax credit rules of paragraph 3 of Article 23 (Relief from Double Taxation), as if the Convention had not come into force.

As with other benefits of the Convention, a resident of one of the States claiming the benefit of this Article must be entitled to those benefits under the provisions of Article 22 (Limitation on Benefits).

ARTICLE 12 (ROYALTIES)

Article 12 provides rules for residence and source country taxation of royalties. Generally, the Article provides for full residence country taxation of royalties and for limited source state right to tax such income.

Paragraph 1

Paragraph 1 grants to the state of residence of the beneficial owner of royalties the right to tax royalties arising in the other Contracting State.

Paragraph 2

Paragraph 2 grants to the source State the right to tax royalty payments but limits the rate of source State tax if the royalties are beneficially owned by a resident of the other Contracting State. The maximum rate of tax allowed by the source State is 5 percent.

The term "beneficial owner" is not defined in the Convention, and is, therefore, defined as under the internal law of the country imposing tax (i.e., the source country). The beneficial owner of the royalty for purposes of Article 12 is the person to which the royalty income is attributable for tax purposes under the laws of the source State. Thus, if a royalty arising in a Contracting State is received by a nominee or agent that is a resident of the other State on behalf of a person that is not a resident of that other State, the royalty is not entitled to the benefits of this Article. However, a royalty received by a nominee on behalf of a resident of that other State would be entitled to benefits. These limitations are confirmed by paragraph 4 of the OECD Commentaries to Article 12. See also paragraph 24 of the OECD Commentaries to Article 1 (General Scope).

Paragraph 3

The term "royalties" as used in Article 12 is defined in paragraph 3 to include payments of any kind received as a consideration for the use of, or the right to use, any copyright of a literary, artistic, scientific or other work; for the use of, or the right to use, any patent, trademark, design or model, plan, secret formula or process, or other like right or property; or for information concerning industrial, commercial, or scientific experience. It does not include income from leasing personal property.

The term royalties is defined in the Convention and therefore is generally independent of domestic law. Certain terms used in the definition are not defined in the Convention, but these may be defined under domestic tax law. For example, the term "secret process or formulas" is found in the Code, and its meaning has been elaborated in the context of sections 351 and 367. See Rev. Rul. 55-17, 1955-1 C.B. 388; Rev. Rul. 64-56, 1964-1 C.B. 133; Rev. Proc. 69-19, 1969-2 C.B. 301.

Consideration for the use or right to use cinematographic films, or works on film, tape, or other means of reproduction in radio or television broadcasting is specifically included in the definition of royalties. It is intended that subsequent technological advances in the field of radio and television broadcasting will not affect the inclusion of payments relating to the use of such means of reproduction in the definition of royalties.

If an artist who is resident in one Contracting State records a performance in the other Contracting State, retains a copyrighted interest in a recording, and receives payments for the right to use the recording based on the sale or public playing of the recording, then the right of such other Contracting State to tax those payments is governed by Article 12. See Boulez v. Commissioner, 83 T.C. 584 (1984), aff'd, 810 F.2d 209 (D.C. Cir. 1986).

Computer software generally is protected by copyright laws around the world. Under the Convention, consideration received for the use, or the right to use, computer software is treated either as royalties or as business profits, depending on the facts and circumstances of the transaction giving rise to the payment.

The primary factor in determining whether consideration received for the use, or the right to use, computer software is treated as royalties or as business profits, is the nature of the rights transferred. See Treas. Reg. section 1.861-18. The fact that the transaction is characterized as a license for copyright law purposes is not dispositive. For example, as was discussed and understood among the negotiators, a typical retail sale of "shrink wrap" software generally will not be considered to give rise to royalty income, even though for copyright law purposes it may be characterized as a license.

The means by which the computer software is transferred are not relevant for purposes of the analysis. Consequently, if software is electronically transferred but the rights obtained by the transferee are substantially equivalent to rights in a program copy, the payment will be considered business profits.

The term "royalties" also includes gain derived from the alienation of any right or property that would give rise to royalties, to the extent the gain is contingent on the productivity, use, or further alienation thereof. Gains that are not so contingent are dealt with under Article 13 (Gains).

The term "industrial, commercial, or scientific experience" (sometimes referred to as "know-how") has the meaning ascribed to it in paragraph 11 of the Commentary to Article 12 of the OECD Model Convention. Consistent with that meaning, the term may include information that is ancillary to a right otherwise giving rise to royalties, such as a patent or secret process.

Know-how also may include, in limited cases, technical information that is conveyed through technical or consultancy services. It does not include general educational training of the user's employees, nor does it include information developed especially for the user, such as a technical plan or design developed according to the user's specifications. Thus, as provided in paragraph 11 of the Commentaries to Article 12 of the OECD Model, the term "royalties" does not include payments received as consideration for after-sales service, for services rendered by a seller to a purchaser under a guarantee, or for pure technical assistance.

The term "royalties" also does not include payments for professional services (such as architectural, engineering, legal, managerial, medical, software development services). For example, income from the design of a refinery by an engineer (even if the engineer employed know-how in the process of rendering the design) or the production of a legal brief by a lawyer is not income from the transfer of know-how taxable under Article 12, but is income from services taxable under either Article 14 (Independent Personal Services) or Article 15 (Dependent Personal Services). Professional services may be embodied in property that gives rise to royalties, however. Thus, if a professional contracts to develop patentable property and retains rights in the resulting property under the development contract, subsequent license payments made for those rights would be royalties.

Paragraph 4

Paragraph 4 provides an exception to the rules of paragraph 2 that limit the rate of source country taxation of royalties. This paragraph applies in cases where the beneficial owner of the royalties carries on business through a permanent establishment in the state of source or performs independent personal services from a fixed base situated in that state and the royalties are attributable to that permanent establishment or fixed base. In such cases the provisions of Article 7 (Business Profits) or Article 14 (Independent Personal Services) will apply.

The provisions of paragraph 8 of Article 7 (Business Profits) apply to this paragraph. For example, royalty income that is attributable to a permanent establishment or a fixed base and that accrues during the existence of the permanent establishment or fixed base, but is received after the permanent establishment or fixed base no longer exists, remains taxable under the provisions of Articles 7 (Business Profits) or 14 (Independent Personal Services), respectively, and not under this Article.

Paragraph 5

Paragraph 5 provides rules for sourcing royalty payments. Under paragraph 5, royalty payments are deemed to arise in a Contracting State when the payer is that State itself, a political subdivision, a local authority or a resident of that State. However, when the person paying the royalty has a permanent establishment or fixed base in a Contracting State in connection with which the liability to pay the royalty was incurred and the royalty is borne by the permanent establishment or fixed base, then the royalty is deemed to arise in the Contracting State in which the permanent establishment or fixed base is located. This rule applies whether or not the payer is a resident of a Contracting State. Notwithstanding this rule, royalties with respect to the use of, or the right to use, rights or property within a Contracting State may be treated as arising within that Contracting State. For example, if a Slovenian resident were to grant franchise rights to a resident of Mexico for use in the United States, the royalty payment paid by the Mexican resident to the Slovenian resident for those rights would be U.S. source income under this Article, subject to U.S. withholding at the 5 percent rate provided in paragraph 2.

Paragraph 6

Paragraph 6 provides that in cases involving special relationships between the payor and beneficial owner of royalties, Article 12 applies only to the extent the royalties would have been paid absent such special relationships (i.e., an arm's-length royalty). Any excess amount of royalties paid remains taxable according to the laws of the two Contracting States with due regard to the other provisions of the Convention. If, for example, the excess amount is treated as a distribution of corporate profits under domestic law, such excess amount will be taxed as a dividend rather than as royalties, but the tax imposed on the dividend payment will be subject to the rate limitations of paragraph 2 of Article 10 (Dividends).

Paragraph 7

Paragraph 7 provides that the benefits of this Article will be denied in cases in which the main purpose, or one of the main purposes, for the creation or assignment of the rights in respect of which the royalties are paid is to take advantage of this Article. This provision is analogous to paragraph 10 of Article 10 (Dividends), discussed above.

Relation to Other Articles

Notwithstanding the foregoing limitations on source country taxation of royalties, the saving clause of paragraph 4 of Article 1 (General Scope) permits the United States to tax its residents and citizens, subject to the special foreign tax credit rules of paragraph 3 of Article 23 (Relief from Double Taxation), as if the Convention had not come into force.

As with other benefits of the Convention, the benefits of reduced source State taxation of royalties under paragraph 2 of Article 12 are available to a resident of the other State only if that resident is entitled to those benefits under Article 22 (Limitation on Benefits).

ARTICLE 13 (GAINS)

Article 13 assigns either primary or exclusive taxing jurisdiction over gains from the alienation of property to the State of residence or the State of source and defines the terms necessary to apply the Article.

Paragraph 1

Paragraph 1 of Article 13 preserves the non-exclusive right of the State of source to tax gains attributable to the alienation of real property situated in that State. The paragraph therefore permits the United States to apply section 897 of the Code to tax gains derived by a resident of Slovenia that are attributable to the alienation of real property situated in the United States (as defined in paragraph 2). Gains attributable to the alienation of real property include gain from any other property that is treated as a real property interest within the meaning of paragraph 2.

Paragraph 2

This paragraph defines the term "real property situated in the other Contracting State." The term includes real property referred to in Article 6 (i.e., an interest in the real property itself) as well as shares (or other comparable rights, other than shares that are regularly traded on an established securities market) in a company that is a resident of the other Contracting State and that derives at least 50 percent of its value directly or indirectly from immovable (real) property situated in that other State, and an interest in a partnership, trust or estate to the extent that its assets consist of immovable (real) property situated in that other State. This bilateral provision is intended to cover U.S. real property interests as well as any similar interests in Slovenian real property. In applying paragraph 1 the United States will look through distributions made by a REIT. Accordingly, distributions made by a REIT are taxable under paragraph 1 of Article 13 (not under Article 10 (Dividends)) when they are attributable to gains derived from the alienation of real property. The OECD Model does not refer to real property interests other than the real property itself, and the United States has entered a reservation on this point with respect to the OECD Model, reserving the right to apply its tax under FIRPTA to all real estate gains encompassed by that provision.

Paragraph 3

Paragraph 3 of Article 13 deals with the taxation of certain gains from the alienation of personal (movable) property forming part of the business property of a permanent establishment that an enterprise of a Contracting State has in the other Contracting State or of personal (movable) property pertaining to a fixed base available to a resident of a Contracting State in the other Contracting State for the purpose of performing independent personal services. This also includes gains from the alienation of such a permanent establishment (alone or with the whole enterprise) or of such fixed base. Such gains may be taxed in the State in which the permanent establishment or fixed base is located.

A resident of Slovenia that is a partner in a partnership doing business in the United States generally will have a permanent establishment in the United States as a result of the activities of the partnership, assuming that the activities of the partnership rise to the level of a permanent establishment. Rev. Rul. 91-32, 1991-1 C.B. 107. Further, under paragraph 3, the United States generally may tax a partner's distributive share of income realized by a partnership on the disposition of personal (movable) property forming part of the business property of the partnership in the United States.

Paragraph 8 of Article 7 (Business Profits) refers to paragraph 3 of Article 13. That rule clarifies that income that is attributable to a permanent establishment or a fixed base, but that is deferred and received after the permanent establishment or fixed base no longer exists, may nevertheless be taxed by the State in which the permanent establishment or fixed base was located. Thus, under Article 13, gains derived by a resident of a Contracting State from the sale of personal (movable) property forming part of the business property of a permanent establishment in the other Contracting State may be taxed by that other State even if the income is deferred and received after the permanent establishment no longer exists.

Paragraph 4

This paragraph limits the taxing jurisdiction of the state of source with respect to gains from the alienation of ships, aircraft, or containers operated in international traffic or movable property pertaining to the operation of such ships, aircraft, or containers. Under paragraph 4 when such income is derived by an enterprise of a Contracting State it is taxable only in that Contracting State. Notwithstanding paragraph 3, the rules of this paragraph apply even if the income is attributable to a permanent establishment maintained by the enterprise in the other Contracting State. This result is consistent with the general rule under Article 8 (Shipping and Air Transport) that confers exclusive taxing rights over international shipping and air transport income on the state of residence of the enterprise deriving such income.

Paragraph 5

Paragraph 5 grants to the State of residence of the alienator the exclusive right to tax gains from the alienation of property other than property referred to in paragraphs 1 through 4. For example, gain derived from shares, other than shares described in paragraphs 2 or 3, debt instruments and various financial instruments, may be taxed only in the State of residence, to the extent such income is not otherwise characterized as income taxable under another article (e.g., Article 10 (Dividends) or Article 11 (Interest)).   Similarly, gain derived from the alienation of tangible personal property, other than tangible personal property described in paragraph 3, may be taxed only in the State of residence of the alienator. Gain derived from the alienation of any property, such as a patent or copyright, that produces income taxable under Article 12 (Royalties) is taxable under Article 12 and not under this article, provided that such gain is of the type described in subparagraph 3(b) of Article 12 (i.e., it is contingent on the productivity, use, or disposition of the property). Sales by a resident of a Contracting State of real property located in a third state are not taxable in the other Contracting State, even if the sale is attributable to a permanent establishment located in the other Contracting State.

Relation to Other Articles

Notwithstanding the foregoing limitations on taxation of certain gains by the State of source, the saving clause of paragraph 4 of Article 1 (General Scope) permits the United States to tax its citizens and residents as if the Convention had not come into effect. Thus, any limitation in this Article on the right of the United States to tax gains does not apply to gains of a U.S. citizens or resident. The benefits of this Article are also subject to the provisions of Article 22 (Limitation on Benefits). Thus, only a resident of a Contracting State that satisfies one of the conditions in Article 22 is entitled to the benefits of this Article.

ARTICLE 14 (INDEPENDENT PERSONAL SERVICES)

The Convention deals in separate articles with different classes of income from personal services. Article 14 deals with the general class of income from independent personal services and Article 15 deals with the general class of income from dependent personal services. Articles 16 through 20 provide exceptions and additions to these general rules for directors' fees (Article 16); performance income of artistes and sportsmen (Article 17); pensions in respect of personal service income, social security benefits, annuities, alimony, and child support payments (Article 18); government service salaries and pensions (Article 19); and certain income of students, trainees, professors and researchers (Article 20).

Paragraph 1

Paragraph 1 of Article 14 provides the general rule that an individual who is a resident of a Contracting State and who derives income from performing personal services in an independent capacity will be exempt from tax in respect of that income by the other Contracting State. The income may be taxed in the other Contracting State only if the income is attributable to a fixed base that is regularly available to the individual in that other State for the purpose of performing his services.

Income derived by persons other than individuals or groups of individuals from the performance of independent personal services is not covered by Article 14. Such income generally would be business profits taxable in accordance with Article 7 (Business Profits). Income derived by employees of such persons generally would be taxable in accordance with Article 15 (Dependent Personal Services).

The term "fixed base" is not defined in the Convention, but its meaning is understood to be similar, but not identical, to that of the term "permanent establishment," as defined in Article 5 (Permanent Establishment). The term "regularly available" also is not defined in the Convention. Whether a fixed base is regularly available to a person will be determined based on all the facts and circumstances. In general, the term encompasses situations where a fixed base is at the disposal of the individual whenever he performs services in that State. It is not necessary that the individual regularly use the fixed base, only that the fixed base be regularly available to him. For example, a U.S. resident partner in a law firm that has offices in Slovenia would be considered to have a fixed base regularly available to him in Slovenia, if work space in those offices (whether or not the same space) were made available to him whenever he wished to conduct business in Slovenia, regardless of how frequently he conducted business in Slovenia. On the other hand, an individual who had no office in Slovenia and occasionally rented a hotel room to serve as a temporary office would not be considered to have a fixed base regularly available to him.

It is not necessary that the individual actually use the fixed base. It is only necessary that the fixed base be regularly available to him. For example, if an individual has an office in the other State that he can use if he chooses when he is present in the other State, that fixed base will be considered to be regularly available to him regardless of whether he conducts his activities there.

The taxing right conferred by this Article with respect to income from independent personal services can be more limited than that provided in Article 7 for the taxation of business profits. In both articles the income of a resident of one Contracting State must be attributable to a permanent establishment or fixed base in the other State in order for that other State to have a taxing right. In Article 14 the income also must be attributable to services performed in that other State, while Article 7 does not require that all of the income-generating activities be performed in the State where the permanent establishment is located.

This Article applies to income derived by a partner resident in the Contracting State that is attributable to personal services of an independent character performed in the other State through a partnership that has a fixed base in that other Contracting State. Income which may be taxed under this Article includes all income attributable to the fixed base in respect of the performance of the personal services carried on by the partnership (whether by the partner himself, other partners in the partnership, or by employees assisting the partners) and any income from activities ancillary to the performance of those services (for example, charges for facsimile services). Income that is not derived from the performance of personal services and that is not ancillary thereto (for example, rental income from subletting office space), will be governed by other Articles of the Convention.

The application of Article 14 to a service partnership may be illustrated by the following example: a partnership formed in the Contracting State has five partners (who agree to split profits equally), four of whom are resident and perform personal services only in the Contracting State at Office A, and one of whom performs personal services from Office B, a fixed base in the other State. In this case, the four partners of the partnership resident in the Contracting State may be taxed in the other State in respect of their share of the income attributable to the fixed base, Office B. The services giving rise to income which may be attributed to the fixed base would include not only the services performed by the one resident partner, but also, for example, if one of the four other partners came to the other State and worked on an Office B matter there, the income in respect of those services also. As noted above, this would be the case regardless of whether the partner from the Contracting State actually visited or used Office B when performing services in the other State.

Paragraph 8 of Article 7 (Business Profits) refers to Article 14. That rule clarifies that income that is attributable to a permanent establishment or a fixed base, but that is deferred and received after the permanent establishment or fixed base no longer exists, may nevertheless be taxed by the State in which the permanent establishment or fixed base was located. Thus, under Article 14, income derived by an individual resident of a Contracting State from services performed in the other Contracting State and attributable to a fixed base there may be taxed by that other State even if the income is deferred and received after there is no longer a fixed base available to the resident in that other State.

Paragraph 2

Paragraph 2 notes that the term "professional services" includes independent scientific, literary, artistic, educational or teaching activities, as well as the independent activities of physicians, lawyers, engineers, architects, dentists, and accountants. This list, which is derived from the OECD Model, is not exhaustive. The term includes all personal services performed by an individual for his own account, where he receives the income and bears the risk of loss arising from the services. The taxation of income from the types of independent services that are covered by Articles 16 through 20 is governed by the provisions of those articles. For example, taxation of the income of a corporate director would be governed by Article 16 (Directors' Fees) rather than Article 14.

Paragraph 3

This paragraph incorporates the principles of paragraph 3 of Article 7 (Business Profits) into Article 14. Thus, all relevant expenses, including expenses not incurred in the Contracting State where the fixed base is located, must be allowed as deductions in computing the net income from services subject to tax in the Contracting State where the fixed base is located.

Relation to other Articles

If an individual resident of Slovenia who is also a U.S. citizen performs independent personal services in the United States, the United States may, by virtue of the saving clause of paragraph 4 of Article 1 (General Scope) tax his income without regard to the restrictions of this Article, subject to the special foreign tax credit rules of paragraph 3 of Article 23 (Relief from Double Taxation).

ARTICLE 15 (DEPENDENT PERSONAL SERVICES)

Article 15 apportions taxing jurisdiction over remuneration derived by a resident of a Contracting State as an employee between the States of source and residence.

Paragraph 1

The general rule of Article 15 is contained in paragraph 1. Remuneration derived by a resident of a Contracting State as an employee may be taxed by the State of residence, and the remuneration also may be taxed by that other Contracting State to the extent derived from employment exercised (i.e., services performed) in the other Contracting State. Paragraph 1 also provides that the more specific rules of Articles 16 (Directors' Fees), 18 (Pensions, Social Security, Annuities, Alimony and Child Support), and 19 (Government Service) apply in the case of employment income described in one of these articles. Thus, even though the State of source has a right to tax employment income under Article 15, it may not have the right to tax that income under the Convention if the income is described, e.g., in Article 18 (Pensions, Social Security, Annuities, Alimony and Child Support) and is not taxable in the State of source under the provisions of that article.

Article 15 applies to "salaries, wages and other similar remuneration." The U.S. Model has deleted the word "similar." Even with the inclusion of the word "similar," Article 15 should be understood to apply to any form of compensation for employment, including payments in kind, regardless of whether the remuneration is "similar" to salaries and wages. The U.S. position on in-kind payments was confirmed by the addition of paragraph 2.1 to the Commentaries to Article 15 of the OECD Model in 1997.

Consistently with section 864(c)(6), Article 15 also applies regardless of the timing of actual payment for services. Thus, a bonus paid to a resident of a Contracting State with respect to services performed in the other Contracting State with respect to a particular taxable year would be subject to Article 15 for that year even if it was paid after the close of the year. Similarly, an annuity received for services performed in a taxable year would be subject to Article 15 despite the fact that it was paid in subsequent years. In either case, whether such payments were taxable in the State where the employment was exercised would depend on whether the tests of paragraph 2 were satisfied. Consequently, a person who receives the right to a future payment in consideration for services rendered in a Contracting State would be taxable in that State even if the payment is received at a time when the recipient is a resident of the other Contracting State.

Paragraph 2

Paragraph 2 sets forth an exception to the general rule that employment income may be taxed in the State where the employment is exercised. Under paragraph 2, the State where the employment is exercised may not tax the income from the employment if three conditions are satisfied: (a) the individual is present in the other Contracting State for a period or periods not exceeding 183 days in any 12-month period that begins or ends during the relevant (i.e., the year in which the services are performed) calendar year; (b) the remuneration is paid by, or on behalf of, an employer who is not a resident of that other Contracting State; and (c) the remuneration is not borne by a permanent establishment or fixed base that the employer has in that other State. In order for the remuneration to be exempt from tax in the source State, all three conditions must be satisfied. This exception is identical to that set forth in the U.S. and OECD Models.

The 183-day period in condition (a) is to be measured using the "days of physical presence" method. Under this method, the days that are counted include any day in which a part of the day is spent in the host country. (Rev. Rul. 56-24, 1956-1 C.B. 851.) Thus, days that are counted include the days of arrival and departure; weekends and holidays on which the employee does not work but is present within the country; vacation days spent in the country before, during or after the employment period, unless the individual's presence before or after the employment can be shown to be independent of his presence there for employment purposes; and time during periods of sickness, training periods, strikes, etc., when the individual is present but not working. If illness prevented the individual from leaving the country in sufficient time to qualify for the benefit, those days will not count. Also, any part of a day spent in the host country while in transit between two points outside the host country is not counted. These rules are consistent with the description of the 183-day period in paragraph 5 of the Commentary to Article 15 in the OECD Model.

Conditions (b) and (c) are intended to ensure that a Contracting State will not be required to allow a deduction to the payor for compensation paid and at the same time to exempt the employee on the amount received. Accordingly, if a foreign person pays the salary of an employee who is employed in the host State, but a host State corporation or permanent establishment reimburses the payor with a payment that can be identified as a reimbursement, neither condition (b) nor (c), as the case may be, will be considered to have been fulfilled.

The reference to remuneration "borne by" a permanent establishment or fixed base is understood to encompass all expenses that economically are incurred and not merely expenses that are currently deductible for tax purposes. Accordingly, the expenses referred to include expenses that are capitalizable as well as those that are currently deductible. Further, salaries paid by residents that are exempt from income taxation may be considered to be borne by a permanent establishment or fixed base notwithstanding the fact that the expenses will be neither deductible nor capitalizable since the payor is exempt from tax.

Paragraph 3

Paragraph 3 contains a special rule applicable to remuneration for services performed by a resident of a Contracting State as an employee aboard a ship or aircraft operated in international traffic. Such remuneration may be taxed only in the State of residence of the employee if the services are performed as a member of the regular complement of the ship or aircraft. The "regular complement" includes the crew. In the case of a cruise ship, for example, it may also include others, such as entertainers, lecturers, etc., employed by the shipping company to serve on the ship throughout its voyage. The use of the term "regular complement" is intended to clarify that a person who exercises his employment as, for example, an insurance salesman while aboard a ship or aircraft is not covered by this paragraph. This paragraph is inapplicable to persons dealt with in Article 14 (Independent Personal Services).

Relation to other Articles

If a U.S. citizen who is resident in Slovenia performs services as an employee in the United States and meets the conditions of paragraph 2 for source country exemption, he nevertheless is taxable in the United States by virtue of the saving clause of paragraph 4 of Article 1 (General Scope), subject to the special foreign tax credit rule of paragraph 3 of Article 23 (Relief from Double Taxation).

ARTICLE 16 (DIRECTORS' FEES)

This Article provides that a Contracting State may tax the fees and other compensation paid by a company that is a resident of that State for services performed in that State by a resident of the other Contracting State in his capacity as a director of the company. This rule is an exception to the more general rules of Article 14 (Independent Personal Services) and Article 15 (Dependent Personal Services). Thus, for example, in determining whether a director's fee paid to a non-employee director is subject to tax in the country of residence of the corporation, it is not relevant to establish whether the fee is attributable to a fixed base in that State.

The analogous OECD provision reaches a different result in certain cases. Under the OECD Model provision, a resident of one Contracting State who is a director of a corporation that is resident in the other Contracting State is subject to tax in that other State in respect of his directors' fees regardless of where the services are performed. The United States has entered a reservation with respect to the OECD provision. Under this Convention, the State of residence of the corporation may tax nonresident directors with no time or dollar threshold, but only with respect to remuneration for services performed in that State.

This Article is subject to the saving clause of paragraph 4 of Article 1 (General Scope). Thus, if a U.S. citizen who is a resident of Slovenia is a director of a U.S. corporation, the United States may tax his full remuneration regardless of where he performs his services.

ARTICLE 17 (ARTISTES AND SPORTSMEN)

This Article deals with the taxation in a Contracting State of artistes (i.e., performing artists and entertainers) and sportsmen resident in the other Contracting State from the performance of their services as such. The Article applies both to the income of an entertainer or sportsman who performs services on his own behalf and one who performs services on behalf of another person, either as an employee of that person, or pursuant to any other arrangement. The rules of this Article take precedence, in some circumstances, over those of Articles 14 (Independent Personal Services) and 15 (Dependent Personal Services).

This Article applies only with respect to the income of performing artists and sportsmen. Others involved in a performance or athletic event, such as producers, directors, technicians, managers, coaches, etc., remain subject to the provisions of Articles 14 and 15. In addition, except as provided in paragraph 2, income earned by juridical persons is not covered by Article 17.

Paragraph 1

Paragraph 1 describes the circumstances in which a Contracting State may tax the performance income of an entertainer or sportsman who is a resident of the other Contracting State. Under the paragraph, income derived by an individual resident of a Contracting State from activities as an entertainer or sportsman exercised in the other Contracting State may be taxed in that other State if the amount of the gross receipts derived by the performer exceeds $15,000 (or its equivalent in Slovenian tolars) for the taxable year. The $15,000 includes expenses reimbursed to the individual or borne on his behalf. If the gross receipts exceed $15,000, the full amount, not just the excess, may be taxed in the State of performance.

The OECD Model provides for taxation by the country of performance of the remuneration of entertainers or sportsmen with no dollar or time threshold. This Convention introduces the dollar threshold test to distinguish between two groups of entertainers and athletes -- those who are paid relatively large sums of money for very short periods of service, and who would, therefore, normally be exempt from host country tax under the standard personal services income rules, and those who earn relatively modest amounts and are, therefore, not easily distinguishable from those who earn other types of personal service income. The United States has entered a reservation to the OECD Model on this point.

Tax may be imposed under paragraph 1 even if the performer would have been exempt from tax under Articles 14 (Independent Personal Services) or 15 (Dependent Personal Services). On the other hand, if the performer would be exempt from host-country tax under Article 17, but would be taxable under either Article 14 or 15, tax may be imposed under either of those Articles. Thus, for example, if a performer derives remuneration from his activities in an independent capacity, and the remuneration is not attributable to a fixed base, he may be taxed by the host State in accordance with Article 17 if his remuneration exceeds $15,000 annually, despite the fact that he generally would be exempt from host State taxation under Article 14. However, a performer who receives less than the $15,000 threshold amount and therefore is not taxable under Article 17, nevertheless may be subject to tax in the host country under Articles 14 or 15 if the tests for host-country taxability under those Articles are met. For example, if an entertainer who is an independent contractor earns $14,000 of income in a State for the calendar year, but the income is attributable to a fixed base regularly available to him in the State of performance, that State may tax his income under Article 14.

Since it frequently is not possible to know until year-end whether the income an entertainer or sportsman derived from performances in a Contracting State will exceed $15,000, nothing in the Convention precludes that Contracting State from withholding tax during the year and refunding after the close of the year if the taxability threshold has not been met.

As explained in paragraph 9 of the OECD Commentaries to Article 17, Article 17 applies to all income connected with a performance by the entertainer, such as appearance fees, award or prize money, and a share of the gate receipts. Income derived from a Contracting State by a performer who is a resident of the other Contracting State from other than actual performance, such as royalties from record sales and payments for product endorsements, is not covered by this Article, but by other articles of the Convention, such as Article 12 (Royalties) or Article 14 (Independent Personal Services). For example, if an entertainer receives royalty income from the sale of live recordings, the royalty income could be taxed by the source country under Article 12 and he also could be taxed in the source country with respect to income from the performance itself under this Article if the dollar threshold is exceeded.

In determining whether income falls under Article 17 or another article, the controlling factor will be whether the income in question is predominantly attributable to the performance itself or other activities or property rights. For instance, a fee paid to a performer for endorsement of a performance in which the performer will participate would be considered to be so closely associated with the performance itself that it normally would fall within Article 17. Similarly, a sponsorship fee paid by a business in return for the right to attach its name to the performance would be so closely associated with the performance that it would fall under Article 17 as well. As indicated in paragraph 9 of the Commentaries to Article 17 of the OECD Model, a cancellation fee would not be considered to fall within Article 17 but would be dealt with under Article 7 (Business Profits), 14 (Independent Personal Services) or 15 (Dependent Personal Services).

As indicated in paragraph 4 of the Commentaries to Article 17 of the OECD Model, where an individual fulfills a dual role as performer and non-performer (such as a player-coach or an actor-director), but his role in one of the two capacities is negligible, the predominant character of the individual's activities should control the characterization of those activities. In other cases there should be an apportionment between the performance-related compensation and other compensation.

Consistently with Article 15 (Dependent Personal Services), Article 17 also applies regardless of the timing of actual payment for services. Thus, a bonus paid to a resident of a

Contracting State with respect to a performance in the other Contracting State with respect to a particular taxable year would be subject to Article 17 for that year even if it was paid after the close of the year.

Paragraph 2

Paragraph 2 is intended to deal with the potential for abuse when a performer's income does not accrue directly to the performer himself, but to another person. Foreign performers frequently perform in the United States as employees of, or under contract with, a company or other person.

The relationship may truly be one of employee and employer, with no abuse of the tax system either intended or realized. On the other hand, the "employer" may, for example, be a company established and owned by the performer, which is merely acting as the nominal income recipient in respect of the remuneration for the performance (a "star company"). The performer may act as an "employee," receive a modest salary, and arrange to receive the remainder of the income from his performance in another form or at a later time. In such case, absent the provisions of paragraph 2, the income arguably could escape host-country tax because the company earns business profits but has no permanent establishment in that country. The performer may largely or entirely escape host-country tax by receiving only a small salary in the year the services are performed, perhaps small enough to place him below the dollar threshold in paragraph 1. The performer might arrange to receive further payments in a later year, when he is not subject to host-country tax, perhaps as deferred salary payments, dividends or liquidating distributions.

Paragraph 2 seeks to prevent this type of abuse while at the same time protecting the taxpayers' rights to the benefits of the Convention when there is a legitimate employee-employer relationship between the performer and the person providing his services. Under paragraph 2, when the income accrues to a person other than the performer, and the performer or related persons participate, directly or indirectly, in the receipts or profits of that other person, the income may be taxed in the Contracting State where the performer's services are exercised, without regard to the provisions of the Convention concerning business profits (Article 7), independent personal services (Article 14), or dependent personal services (Article 15). Thus, even if the "employer" has no permanent establishment or fixed base in the host country, its income may be subject to tax there under the provisions of paragraph 2. Taxation under paragraph 2 is on the person providing the services of the performer. This paragraph does not affect the rules of paragraph 1, which apply to the performer himself. The income taxable by virtue of paragraph 2 is reduced to the extent of salary payments to the performer, which fall under paragraph 1.

For purposes of paragraph 2, income is deemed to accrue to another person (i.e., the person providing the services of the performer) if that other person has control over, or the right to receive, gross income in respect of the services of the performer. Direct or indirect participation in the profits of a person may include, but is not limited to, the accrual or receipt of deferred remuneration, bonuses, fees, dividends, partnership income or other income or distributions.

Paragraph 2 does not apply if it is established that neither the performer nor any persons related to the performer participate directly or indirectly in the receipts or profits of the person providing the services of the performer. Assume, for example, that a circus owned by a U.S. corporation performs in Slovenia, and promoters of the performance in Slovenia pay the circus, which, in turn, pays salaries to the circus performers. The circus is determined to have no permanent establishment in Slovenia. Since the circus performers do not participate in the profits of the circus, but merely receive their salaries out of the circus' gross receipts, the circus is protected by Article 7 and its income is not subject to host-country tax. Whether the salaries of the circus performers are subject to host-country tax under this Article depends on whether they exceed the $15,000 threshold in paragraph 1.

Since pursuant to Article 1 (General Scope) the Convention only applies to persons who are residents of one of the Contracting States, if the star company is not a resident of one of the Contracting States then taxation of the income is not affected by Article 17 or any other provision of the Convention.

This exception from paragraph 2 for non-abusive cases is not found in the OECD Model. The United States has entered a reservation to the OECD Model on this point.

Paragraph 3

Paragraph 3 of the Article provides an exception to the rules in paragraphs 1 and 2 in the case of a visit to a Contracting State by an artiste or sportsman who is a resident of the other Contracting State, if the visit is wholly or mainly supported by the public funds of one or both Contracting States or political subdivisions or local authorities of either State. In that case, only the Contracting State of which the artiste or sportsman is a resident may tax his income from those services. Some other recent U.S. treaties, including the treaties with Germany and France, provide a similar exception.

Relationship to other articles

This Article is subject to the provisions of the saving clause of paragraph 4 of Article 1 (General Scope). Thus, if an entertainer or a sportsman who is resident in Slovenia is a citizen of the United States, the United States may tax all of his income from performances in the United States without regard to the provisions of this Article, subject, however, to the special foreign tax credit provisions of paragraph 3 of Article 23 (Relief from Double Taxation). In addition, benefits of this Article are subject to the provisions of Article 22 (Limitation on Benefits).

ARTICLE 18 (PENSIONS, SOCIAL SECURITY, ANNUITIES, ALIMONY, AND CHILD SUPPORT)

This Article deals with the taxation of private (i.e., non-government service) pensions and annuities, social security benefits, alimony and child support payments.

Paragraph 1

Paragraph 1 provides that distributions from pensions and other similar remuneration beneficially owned by a resident of a Contracting State in consideration of past employment are taxable only in the State of residence of the beneficiary. This paragraph makes explicit the fact that the term "pension distributions and other similar remuneration" includes both periodic and lump sum payments.

The phrase "pension distributions and other similar remuneration" is intended to encompass payments made by private retirement plans and arrangements in consideration of past employment. In the United States, the plans encompassed by Paragraph 1 include: qualified plans under section 401(a), individual retirement plans (including individual retirement plans that are part of a simplified employee pension plan that satisfies section 408(k), individual retirement accounts, individual retirement annuities, section 408(p) accounts, and Roth IRAs under section 408A), non-discriminatory section 457 plans, section 403(a) qualified annuity plans, and section 403(b) plans. The competent authorities may agree that distributions from other plans that generally meet similar criteria to those applicable to other plans established under their respective laws also qualify for the benefits of Paragraph 1. In the United States, these criteria are as follows:

a) The plan must be written;

b) In the case of an employer-maintained plan, the plan must be nondiscriminatory insofar as it (alone or in combination with other comparable plans) must cover a wide range of employees. including rank and file employees, and actually provide significant benefits for the entire range of covered employees;

c) In the case of an employer-maintained plan the plan must contain provisions that severely limit the employees' ability to use plan assets for purposes other than retirement, and in all cases be subject to tax provisions that discourage participants from using the assets for purposes other than retirement; and

d) The plan must provide for payment of a reasonable level of benefits at death, a stated age, or an event related to work status, and otherwise require minimum distributions under rules designed to ensure that any death benefits provided to the participants' survivors are merely incidental to the retirement benefits provided to the participants.

In addition, certain distribution requirements must be met before distributions from these plans would fall under paragraph 1. To qualify as a pension distribution or similar remuneration from a U.S. plan the employee must have been either employed by the same employer for five years or be at least 62 years old at the time of the distribution. In addition, the distribution must be made either (A) on account of death or disability, (B) as part of a series of substantially equal payments over the employee's life expectancy (or over the joint life expectancy of the employee and a beneficiary), or (C) after the employee attained the age of 55. Finally, the distribution must be made either after separation from service or on or after attainment of age 65. A distribution from a pension plan solely due to termination of the pension plan is not a distribution falling under paragraph 1.

Pensions in respect of government service are not covered by this paragraph. They are covered either by paragraph 2 of this Article, if they are in the form of social security benefits, or by paragraph 2 of Article 19 (Government Service). Thus, Article 19 covers section 457, 401(a) and 403(b) plans established for government employees. If a pension in respect of government service is not covered by Article 19 solely because the service is not "in the discharge of functions of a governmental nature," the pension is covered by this article.

The exclusive residence-based taxation provided under this paragraph is limited to taxation of amounts that were not previously included in taxable income in the other Contracting State. For example, if a Contracting State had imposed tax on the resident with respect to some portion of a pension plan's earnings, subsequent distributions to a resident of the other State would not be taxable in that State to the extent the distributions were attributable to such amounts. In determining the amount of a distribution that is attributable to previously taxed amounts, the ordering rules of the residence State will be applied. The United States will treat any amount that has increased the recipient's "investment in the contract" (as defined in section 72) as having been previously included in taxable income.

Paragraph 2

The treatment of social security benefits is dealt with in paragraph 2. This paragraph provides that, notwithstanding the provision of paragraph 1 under which private pensions are taxable exclusively in the State of residence of the beneficial owner, payments made by one of the Contracting States under the provisions of its social security or similar legislation to a resident of Slovenia or to a citizen of the United States will be taxable only in the Contracting State making the payment. This paragraph applies to social security beneficiaries whether they have contributed to the system as private sector or Government employees.

The phrase "similar legislation" is intended to refer to United States tier 1 Railroad Retirement benefits. The reference to U.S. citizens is necessary to ensure that a social security payment by Slovenia to a U.S. citizen who is not resident in the United States will not be taxable by the United States.

Paragraph 3

Under paragraph 3, annuities that are derived and beneficially owned by a resident of a Contracting State are taxable only in that State. An annuity, as the term is used in this paragraph, means a stated sum paid periodically at stated times during a specified number of years or for life, under an obligation to make the payment in return for adequate and full consideration (other than for services rendered). An annuity received in consideration for services rendered would be treated as deferred compensation and generally taxable in accordance with Article 14 (Independent Personal Services) or Article 15 (Dependent Personal Services).

Paragraphs 4 and 5

Paragraphs 4 and 5 deal with alimony and child support payments. Both alimony, under paragraph 4, and child support payments, under paragraph 5, are defined as periodic payments made pursuant to a written separation agreement or a decree of divorce, separate maintenance, or compulsory support. Paragraph 4, however, deals only with payments of that type that are deductible to the payor and taxable to the payee. Under that paragraph, alimony (i.e., a deductible payment that is taxable in the hands of the recipient) paid by a resident of a Contracting State to a resident of the other Contracting State is taxable under the Convention only in the State of residence of the recipient. Paragraph 5 deals with those periodic payments that are for the support of a child and that are not covered by paragraph 4 (i.e., those payments that either are not deductible to the payor or not taxable to the payee). These types of payments by a resident of a Contracting State to a resident of the other Contracting State are taxable in neither Contracting State.

Relationship to other Articles

Paragraphs 1, 3 and 4 of Article 18 are subject to the saving clause of paragraph 4 of Article 1 (General Scope). Thus, a U.S. citizen who is resident in Slovenia, and receives either a pension, annuity or alimony payment from the United States, may be subject to U.S. tax on the payment, notwithstanding the rules in those three paragraphs that give the State of residence of the recipient the exclusive taxing right. Paragraphs 2 and 5, however, are excepted from the saving clause by virtue of paragraph 5(a) of Article 1. Thus, the United States will allow U.S. citizens and residents the benefits of paragraphs 2 and 5.

ARTICLE 19 (GOVERNMENT SERVICE)

Paragraph 1

Subparagraphs (a) and (b) of paragraph 1 deal with the taxation of government compensation (other than a pension addressed in paragraph 2). Subparagraph (a) provides that remuneration paid from the public funds of one of the States or its political subdivisions or local authorities to any individual who is rendering services to that State, political subdivision or local authority, which are in the discharge of governmental functions, is exempt from tax by the other State. Under subparagraph (b), such payments are, however, taxable exclusively in the other State (i.e., the host State) if the services are rendered in that other State and the individual is a resident of that State who is either a national of that State or a person who did not become resident of that State solely for purposes of rendering the services. Unlike the OECD Model, the paragraph applies both to government employees and to independent contractors engaged by governments to perform services for them.

The remuneration described in paragraph 1 is subject to the provisions of this paragraph and not to those of Articles 14 (Independent Personal Services), 15 (Dependent Personal Services), 16 (Director's Fees) or 17 (Artistes and Sportsmen). If, however, the conditions of paragraph 1 are not satisfied, those other Articles will apply. Thus, if a local government runs a business, even though the employees who are working for the business are employees of the local government, the compensation of those employees is covered by Article 15 and not Article 19, because the employees are not engaging in a governmental function when they perform their employment duties. Further, the remuneration of artists or sportsmen who are performing in one Contracting State and are sponsored by the government of the other Contracting State is taxable under paragraph 3 of Article 17 (Artistes and Sportsmen) only in the State sponsoring the performance. Such remuneration is not taxable under this Article because such performers are not employees of the government nor are they discharging functions of a governmental nature.

Paragraph 2

Paragraph 2 deals with the taxation of a pension paid from the public funds of one of the States or a political subdivision or a local authority thereof to an individual in respect of services rendered to that State or subdivision or authority in the discharge of governmental functions. Subparagraph (a) provides that such a pension is taxable only in that State. Subparagraph (b) provides an exception under which such a pension is taxable only in the other State if the individual is a resident of, and a national of, that other State. Pensions paid to retired civilian and military employees of a Government of either State are intended to be covered under paragraph 2. When benefits paid by a State in respect of services rendered to that State or a subdivision or authority are in the form of social security benefits, however, those payments are covered by paragraph 2 of Article 18 (Pensions, Social Security, Annuities, Alimony, and Child Support). As a general matter, the result will be the same whether Article 18 or 19 applies, since social security benefits are taxable exclusively by the source country and so are government pensions. The result will differ only when the payment is made to a citizen and resident of the other Contracting State, who is not also a citizen of the paying State. In such a case, social security benefits continue to be taxable at source while government pensions become taxable only in the residence country.

The phrase "functions of a governmental nature" is not defined. In general it is understood to encompass functions traditionally carried on by a government. Generally, it would not include functions that commonly are found in the private sector (e.g., education, health care, utilities). Rather, it is limited to functions that generally are carried on solely by the government (e.g., military, diplomatic service, tax administrators) and activities that directly support the carrying out of those functions.

The use of the phrase "paid from the public funds of a Contracting State" is intended to clarify that remuneration and pensions paid by such entities as government-owned corporations are covered by the Article, as long as the other conditions of the Article are satisfied.

Relation to other Articles

Under paragraph 5(b) of Article 1 (General Scope), the saving clause (paragraph 4 of Article 1) does not apply to the benefits conferred by one of the States under Article 19 if the recipient of the benefits is neither a citizen of that State, nor a person who has been admitted for permanent residence there (i.e., in the United States, a "green card" holder). Thus, a resident of a Contracting State who in the course of performing functions of a governmental nature becomes a resident of the other State (but not a permanent resident), would be entitled to the benefits of this Article. However, an individual who receives a pension paid by the Government of the other Contracting State in respect of services rendered to that Government is taxable on that pension only in the other Contracting State unless the individual is a U.S. citizen or acquires a U.S. green card.

ARTICLE 20 (STUDENTS, TRAINEES, TEACHERS AND RESEARCHERS)

Paragraph 1

Paragraph 1(a) of Article 20 provides that a resident of a Contracting State who visits the other Contracting State for the primary purpose of studying at a university or other recognized educational institution, securing training in a professional specialty, or studying or engaging in research of an educational nature shall be exempt from taxation in that Contracting State with respect to certain items of income during such period of study, research, or training. Paragraph 1(b) defines those exempt items of income as 1) payments from abroad, other than compensation for personal services, for maintenance, education, study, research, or training; 2) grants, allowances, or awards from a governmental, religious, charitable, scientific, literary, or educational institution funding the research or studies; and 3) income from personal services performed in that other Contracting State not in excess of $5,000 (or the equivalent in Slovenian tolars) per taxable year. The exemptions provided in paragraph 1 are available to the visiting student or trainee for a period not exceeding five years from the beginning of the visit, and for such additional period of time as is necessary to complete, as a full-time student, educational requirements as a candidate for a postgraduate or professional degree from a recognized educational institution.

Paragraph 2

Paragraph 2 provides an exemption for residents of a Contracting State who are employed by, or under contract with, a resident of the same Contracting State and who temporarily visit the other Contracting State for the purpose of studying at a university or other recognized educational institution or acquiring technical, professional, or business training or experience in that other Contracting State, provided such training is from a person other than the employer or contractor. Such student or trainee is exempt from taxation in the other Contracting State for a period of twelve months on personal services income not in excess of $8,000 (or the equivalent in Slovenian tolars) during that period.

Paragraph 3

Paragraph 3 provides a limited exemption from tax in a Contracting State for income from personal services of individuals resident in the other Contracting State, who are temporarily present in the first-mentioned State for the purpose of teaching or carrying on research at a recognized educational or research institution in that first State. Unlike the exemptions provided in paragraphs 1 and 2, paragraph 3 provides no dollar limit to these benefits for teachers and researchers. However, paragraph 3 does establish that the host country exemption provided shall last only two years from the date of entry of that individual in the host State, and in no case shall the benefits of the paragraph be granted for more than five taxable years to any individual.

Paragraph 4

Paragraph 4 establishes that the exemptions provided in this Article do not apply to income from research if such research is undertaken primarily for the private benefit of a specific person or persons. For example, personal service income arising from research at a corporate research facility would, in general, not qualify as exempt income.

Relation to other articles

Under paragraph 5(b) of Article 1 (General Scope), the saving clause of paragraph 4 of Article 1 does not apply to this Article with respect to an individual who is neither a citizen of the host State nor has been admitted for permanent residence there. The saving clause, however, does apply with respect to citizens and permanent residents of the host State. Thus, a U.S. citizen who is a resident of Slovenia and who visits the United States as a full-time student at an accredited university will not be exempt from U.S. tax on remittances from abroad that otherwise constitute U.S. taxable income. A person, however, who is not a U.S. citizen, and who visits the United States as a student and remains long enough to become a resident under U.S. law, but does not become a permanent resident (i.e. does not acquire a green card), will be entitled to full benefits of the Article.

ARTICLE 21 (OTHER INCOME)

Article 21 generally assigns taxing jurisdiction over income not dealt with in the other articles (Articles 6 through 20) of the Convention to the State of residence of the beneficial owner of the income and defines the terms necessary to apply the article. An item of income is "dealt with" in another article if it is the type of income described in the article and it has its source in a Contracting State. For example, all royalty income that arises in a Contracting State and that is beneficially owned by a resident of the other Contracting State is "dealt with" in Article 12 (Royalties).

Examples of items of income covered by Article 21 include income from gambling, punitive (but not compensatory) damages, covenants not to compete, and income from certain financial instruments to the extent derived by persons not engaged in the trade or business of dealing in such instruments (unless the transaction giving rise to the income is related to a trade or business, in which case it is dealt with under Article 7 (Business Profits)). The article also applies to items of income that are not dealt with in the other articles because of their source or some other characteristic. For example, Article 11 (Interest) addresses only the taxation of interest arising in a Contracting State. Interest arising in a third State that is not attributable to a permanent establishment, therefore, is subject to Article 21.

Distributions from partnerships and distributions from trusts are not generally dealt with under Article 21 because partnership and trust distributions generally do not constitute income. Under the Code, partners include in income their distributive share of partnership income annually, and partnership distributions themselves generally do not give rise to income. Also, under the Code, trust income and distributions have the character of the associated distributable net income and therefore would generally be covered by another article of the Convention. See Code section 641 et seq.

Paragraph 1

The general rule of Article 21 is contained in paragraph 1. Items of income not dealt with in other articles and beneficially owned by a resident of a Contracting State will be taxable only in the State of residence. This exclusive right of taxation applies whether or not the residence State exercises its right to tax the income covered by the Article.

The reference in this paragraph to "items of income beneficially owned by a resident of a Contracting State" rather than simply "items of income of a resident of a Contracting State," as in the OECD Model, it is intended merely to make explicit the implicit understanding in other treaties that the exclusive residence taxation provided by paragraph 1 applies only when a resident of a Contracting State is the beneficial owner of the income. Thus, source taxation of income not dealt with in other articles of the Convention is not limited by paragraph 1 if it is nominally paid to a resident of the other Contracting State, but is beneficially owned by a resident of a third State.

Paragraph 2

This paragraph provides an exception to the general rule of paragraph 1 for income, other than income from real property, that is attributable to a permanent establishment or fixed base maintained in a Contracting State by a resident of the other Contracting State. The taxation of such income is governed by the provisions of Articles 7 (Business Profits) and 14 (Independent Personal Services). Therefore, income arising outside the United States that is attributable to a permanent establishment maintained in the United States by a resident of Slovenia generally would be taxable by the United States under the provisions of Article 7. This would be true even if the income is sourced in a third State.

There is an exception to this general rule with respect to income a resident of a Contracting State derives from real property located outside the other Contracting State (whether in the first-mentioned Contracting State or in a third State) that is attributable to the resident's permanent establishment or fixed base in the other Contracting State. In such a case, only the first-mentioned Contracting State (i.e., the State of residence of the person deriving the income) and not the host State of the permanent establishment or fixed base may tax that income. This special rule for foreign-situs property is consistent with the general rule, also reflected in Article 6 (Income from Real Property (Immovable Property)), that only the situs and residence States may tax real property and real property income. Even if such property is part of the property of a permanent establishment or fixed base in a Contracting State, that State may not tax the income if neither the situs of the property nor the residence of the owner is in that State.

Paragraph 3

Paragraph 3 provides that the benefits of this Article will be denied in cases in which the main purpose, or one of the main purposes, for the creation or assignment of the rights in respect of which the income is paid is to take advantage of this Article. This provision is analogous to paragraph 10 of Article 10 (Dividends), discussed above.

Relation to Other Articles

This Article is subject to the saving clause of paragraph 4 of Article 1 (General Scope). Thus, the United States may tax the income of a resident of Slovenia that is not dealt with elsewhere in the Convention, if that resident is a citizen of the United States. The Article is also subject to the provisions of Article 22 (Limitation on Benefits). Thus, if a resident of Slovenia earns income that falls within the scope of paragraph 1 of Article 21, but that is taxable by the United States under U.S. law, the income would be exempt from U.S. tax under the provisions of Article 21 only if the resident satisfies one of the tests of Article 22 for entitlement to benefits.

ARTICLE 22 (LIMITATION ON BENEFITS)

Purpose of Limitation on Benefits Provisions

The United States views an income tax treaty as a vehicle for providing treaty benefits to residents of the two Contracting States. This statement begs the question of who is to be treated as a resident of a Contracting State for the purpose of being granted treaty benefits. The Commentaries to the OECD Model authorize a tax authority to deny benefits, under substance-over-form principles, to a nominee in one State deriving income from the other on behalf of a third-country resident. In addition, although the text of the OECD Model does not contain express anti-abuse provisions, the Commentaries to Article 1 contain an extensive discussion approving the use of such provisions in tax treaties in order to limit the ability of third state residents to obtain treaty benefits. The United States holds strongly to the view that tax treaties should include provisions that specifically prevent misuse of treaties by residents of third countries. Consequently, all recent U.S. income tax treaties contain comprehensive Limitation on Benefits provisions.

A treaty that provides treaty benefits to any resident of a Contracting State permits "treaty shopping": the use, by residents of third states, of legal entities established in a Contracting State with a principal purpose to obtain the benefits of a tax treaty between the United States and the other Contracting State. It is important to note that this definition of treaty shopping does not encompass every case in which a third state resident establishes an entity in a U.S. treaty partner, and that entity enjoys treaty benefits to which the third state resident would not itself be entitled. If the third country resident had substantial reasons for establishing the structure that were unrelated to obtaining treaty benefits, the structure would not fall within the definition of treaty shopping set forth above.

Of course, the fundamental problem presented by this approach is that it is based on the taxpayer's motives in establishing an entity in a particular country, which a tax administrator is normally ill-equipped to identify. In order to avoid the necessity of making this subjective determination, Article 22 sets forth a series of objective tests. The assumption underlying each of these tests is that a taxpayer that satisfies the requirements of any of the tests probably has a real business purpose for the structure it has adopted, or has a sufficiently strong nexus to the other Contracting State (e.g., a resident individual) to warrant benefits even in the absence of a business connection, and that this business purpose or connection is sufficient to justify the conclusion that obtaining the benefits of the treaty is not a principal purpose of establishing or maintaining residence in that other State.

For instance, the assumption underlying the active trade or business test under paragraph 3 is that a third country resident that establishes a "substantial" operation in Slovenia and that derives income from a similar activity in the United States would not do so primarily to avail itself of the benefits of the Treaty; it is presumed in such a case that the investor had a valid business purpose for investing in Slovenia, and that the link between that trade or business and the U.S. activity that generates the treaty-benefitted income manifests a business purpose for placing the U.S. investments in the entity in Slovenia. It is considered unlikely that the investor would incur the expense of establishing a substantial trade or business in Slovenia simply to obtain the benefits of the Convention. A similar rationale underlies other tests in Article 22.

While these tests provide useful surrogates for identifying actual intent, these mechanical tests cannot account for every case in which the taxpayer was not treaty shopping. Accordingly, Article 22 also includes a provision (paragraph 4) authorizing the competent authority of a Contracting State to grant benefits. While an analysis under paragraph 4 may well differ from that under one of the other tests of Article 22, its objective is the same: to identify investors whose residence in the other State can be justified by factors other than a purpose to derive treaty benefits.

Article 22 and the anti-abuse provisions of domestic law complement each other, as Article 22 effectively determines whether an entity has a sufficient nexus to the Contracting State to be treated as a resident for treaty purposes, while domestic anti-abuse provisions (e.g., business purpose, substance-over-form, step transaction or conduit principles) determine whether a particular transaction should be recast in accordance with its substance. Thus, internal law principles of the source State may be applied to identify the beneficial owner of an item of income, and Article 22 then will be applied to the beneficial owner to determine if that person is entitled to the benefits of the Convention with respect to such income.

Even if a resident of a Contracting State is entitled to the benefits of the Convention pursuant to Article 22, other provisions of the Convention may preclude that person from obtaining benefits with respect to specific transactions. In particular, paragraph 10 of Article 10 (Dividends), paragraph 10 of Article 11 (Interest), paragraph 7 of Article 12 (Royalties), or paragraph 3 of Article 21 (Other Income) may deny the benefits of the respective articles in the event of abusive transactions where the main purpose, or one of the main purposes, of the transaction was to take advantage of the relevant article.

Structure of the Article

The structure of the Article is as follows: Paragraph 1 states the general rule that residents are entitled to benefits otherwise accorded to residents only to the extent provided in the Article. Paragraph 2 lists a series of attributes of a resident of a Contracting State, the presence of any one of which will entitle that person to all the benefits of the Convention. Paragraph 3 provides that, with respect to a person not entitled to benefits under paragraph 2, benefits nonetheless may be granted to that person with regard to certain types of income. Paragraph 4 provides that benefits also may be granted if the competent authority of the State from which benefits are claimed determines that it is appropriate to provide benefits in that case. Paragraph 5 defines the term "recognized stock exchange" as used in paragraph 2(c).

Paragraph 1

Paragraph 1 provides that a resident of a Contracting State will be entitled to the benefits otherwise accorded to residents of a Contracting State under the Convention only to the extent provided in the Article. The benefits otherwise accorded to residents under the Convention include all limitations on source-based taxation under Articles 6 through 21, the treaty-based relief from double taxation provided by Article 23 (Relief from Double Taxation), and the protection afforded to residents of a Contracting State under Article 24 (Non-Discrimination). Some provisions do not require that a person be a resident in order to enjoy the benefits of those provisions. These include paragraph 1 of Article 24 (Non-Discrimination), Article 25 (Mutual Agreement Procedure), and Article 27 (Diplomatic Agents and Consular Officers). Article 22 accordingly does not limit the availability of the benefits of these provisions.

Paragraph 2

Paragraph 2 has six subparagraphs, each of which describes a category of residents that are entitled to all benefits of the Convention. It is intended that the provisions of paragraph 2 will be self-executing. Unlike the provisions of paragraph 4, discussed below, claiming benefits under paragraph 2 does not require advance competent authority ruling or approval. The tax authorities may, of course, on review, determine that the taxpayer has improperly interpreted the paragraph and is not entitled to the benefits claimed.

Individuals -- Subparagraph 2(a)

Subparagraph (a) provides that individual residents of a Contracting State will be entitled to all treaty benefits. If such an individual receives income as a nominee on behalf of a third country resident, benefits may be denied under the respective articles of the Convention by the requirement that the beneficial owner of the income be a resident of a Contracting State.

Qualified Governmental Entities -- Subparagraph 2(b)

Subparagraph (b) provides that qualified governmental entities, as defined in subparagraph 1(i) of Article 3 (Definitions), also will be entitled to all benefits of the Convention. As described in Article 3, in addition to federal, state and local governments, the term "qualified governmental entity" encompasses certain government-owned corporations and other entities, and certain pension trusts or funds that administer pension benefits described in Article 19 (Government Service).

Publicly-Traded Corporations -- Subparagraph 2(c)(i)

Subparagraph (c) applies to two categories of corporations: publicly-traded corporations and subsidiaries of publicly-traded corporations. Clause (i) of subparagraph 2(c) provides that a company will be entitled to all the benefits of the Convention if all the shares in the class or classes of shares that represent more than 50 percent of the voting power and value of the company are regularly traded on a "recognized stock exchange" located in either State. The term "recognized stock exchange" is defined in paragraph 5. This language is intended to make it clear that all shares in the principal class or classes of shares (as opposed to only a portion of such shares) must satisfy the requirements of this subparagraph.

If a company has only one class of shares, it is only necessary to consider whether the shares of that class are regularly traded on a recognized stock exchange. If the company has more than one class of shares, it is necessary as an initial matter to determine whether one of the classes accounts for more than half of the voting power and value of the company. If so, then only those shares are considered for purposes of the regular trading requirement. If no single class of shares accounts for more than half of the company's voting power and value, it is necessary to identify a group of two or more classes of the company's shares that account for more than half of the company's voting power and value, and then to determine whether each class of shares in this group satisfies the regular trading requirement. Although in a particular case involving a company with several classes of shares it is conceivable that more than one group of classes could be identified that account for more than 50% of the shares, it is only necessary for one such group to satisfy the requirements of this subparagraph in order for the company to be entitled to benefits.

Benefits would not be denied to the company even if a second, non-qualifying, group of shares with more than half of the company's voting power and value could be identified.

The term "regularly traded" is not defined in the Convention. In accordance with paragraph 2 of Article 3 (General Definitions), this term will be defined by reference to the domestic tax laws of the State from which treaty benefits are sought, generally the source State. In the case of the United States, this term is understood to have the meaning it has under Treas. Reg. section 1.884-5(d)(4)(i)(B), relating to the branch tax provisions of the Code. Under these regulations, a class of shares is considered to be "regularly traded" if two requirements are met: trades in the class of shares are made in more than de minimis quantities on at least 60 days during the taxable year, and the aggregate number of shares in the class traded during the year is at least 10 percent of the average number of shares outstanding during the year. Sections 1.884-5(d)(4)(i)(A), (ii) and (iii) will not be taken into account for purposes of defining the term "regularly traded" under the Convention. Authorized but unissued shares are not considered for purposes of this test.

As described more fully below, the regular trading requirement can be met by trading on any recognized exchange or exchanges located in either State, or if the competent authorities so agree, in a third state. Trading on one or more recognized stock exchanges may be aggregated for purposes of this requirement. Thus, a U.S. company could satisfy the regularly traded requirement through trading, in whole or in part, on a recognized stock exchange located in Slovenia.

Subsidiaries of Publicly-Traded Corporations -- Subparagraph 2(c)(ii)

Clause (ii) of subparagraph 2(c) provides a test under which certain companies that are directly or indirectly controlled by companies satisfying the publicly-traded test of subparagraph 2(c)(i) may be entitled to the benefits of the Convention. Under this test, a company will be entitled to the benefits of the Convention if 50 percent or more of each class of shares in the company is directly or indirectly owned by 5 or fewer companies that are described in subparagraph 2(c)(i).

This test differs from that under subparagraph 2(c)(i) in that 50 percent of each class of the company's shares, not merely the class or classes accounting for more than 50 percent of the company's votes and value, must be held by publicly-traded companies described in subparagraph 2(c)(i). Thus, the test under subparagraph 2(c)(ii) considers the ownership of every class of shares outstanding, while the test under subparagraph 2(c)(i) only considers those classes that account for a majority of the company's voting power and value.

Clause (ii) permits indirect ownership. Consequently, the ownership by publicly-traded companies described in clause (i) need not be direct. However, any intermediate owners in the chain of ownership must themselves be entitled to benefits under paragraph 2.

Tax Exempt Organizations -- Subparagraph 2(d)

Subparagraph 2(d) provides that the tax exempt organizations described in subparagraph 1(c)(i) of Article 4 (Residence) will be entitled to all the benefits of the Convention. These entities are entities that generally are exempt from tax in their State of residence and that are organized and operated exclusively to fulfill religious, charitable, educational, scientific or other similar purposes.

Pension Funds -- Subparagraph 2(e)

Subparagraph 2(e) provides that organizations described in subparagraph 1(c)(ii) of Article 4 (Residence) will be entitled to all the benefits of the Convention, as long as more than half of the beneficiaries, members or participants of the organization are individual residents of either Contracting State. The organizations referred to in this provision are tax-exempt entities that provide pension or other similar benefits to employees pursuant to a plan. For purposes of this provision, the term "beneficiaries" should be understood to refer to the persons receiving benefits from the organization.

Ownership/Base Erosion -- Subparagraph 2(f)

Subparagraph 2(f) provides a two part test, the so-called ownership and base erosion test. This test applies to any form of legal entity that is a resident of a Contracting State. Both prongs of the test must be satisfied for the resident to be entitled to benefits under subparagraph 2(f).

The ownership prong of the test, under clause (i), requires that 50 percent or more of each class of beneficial interests in the person (in the case of a corporation, 50 percent or more of each class of its shares) be owned on at least half the days of the person's taxable year by persons who are themselves entitled to benefits under the other tests of paragraph 2 (i.e., subparagraphs (a), (b), (c), (d), or (e). The ownership may be indirect through other persons themselves entitled to benefits under paragraph 2.

Trusts may be entitled to benefits under this provision if they are treated as residents under Article 4 (Residence) and they otherwise satisfy the requirements of this subparagraph. For purposes of this subparagraph, the beneficial interests in a trust will be considered to be owned by its beneficiaries in proportion to each beneficiary's actuarial interest in the trust. The interest of a remainder beneficiary will be equal to 100 percent less the aggregate percentages held by income beneficiaries. A beneficiary's interest in a trust will not be considered to be owned by a person entitled to benefits under the other provisions of paragraph 2 if it is not possible to determine the beneficiary's actuarial interest. Consequently, if it is not possible to determine the actuarial interest of any beneficiaries in a trust, the ownership test under clause i) cannot be satisfied, unless all beneficiaries are persons entitled to benefits under the other subparagraphs of paragraph 2.

The base erosion prong of the test under clause (ii) requires that less than 50 percent of the person's gross income for the taxable year be paid or accrued, directly or indirectly, to non-residents of either State (unless income is attributable to a permanent establishment located in either Contracting State), in the form of payments that are deductible for tax purposes in the entity's State of residence. To the extent they are deductible from the taxable base, trust distributions would be considered deductible payments. Depreciation and amortization deductions, which are not "payments," are disregarded for this purpose. The purpose of this provision is to determine whether the income derived from the source State is in fact subject to the tax regime of either State. Consequently, payments to any resident of either State, as well as payments that are attributable to permanent establishments in either State, are not considered base eroding payments for this purpose (to the extent that these recipients do not themselves base erode to non-residents).

The term "gross income" is not defined in the Convention. Thus, in accordance with paragraph 2 of Article 3 (General Definitions), in determining whether a person deriving income from United States sources is entitled to the benefits of the Convention, the United States will ascribe the meaning to the term that it has in the United States. In such cases, "gross income" will be defined as gross receipts less cost of goods sold.

Paragraph 3

Paragraph 3 sets forth a test under which a resident of a Contracting State that is not generally entitled to benefits of the Convention under paragraph 2 may receive treaty benefits with respect to certain items of income that are connected to an active trade or business conducted in its State of residence.

Subparagraph 3(a) sets forth a three-pronged test that must be satisfied in order for a resident of a Contracting State to be entitled to the benefits of the Convention with respect to a particular item of income. First, the resident must be engaged in the active conduct of a trade of business in its State of residence. Second, the income derived from the other State must be derived in connection with, or be incidental to, that trade or business. Third, the trade or business must be substantial in relation to the activity in the other State that generated the item of income. These determinations are made separately for each item of income derived from the other State. It therefore is possible that a person would be entitled to the benefits of the Convention with respect to one item of income but not with respect to another. If a resident of a Contracting State is entitled to treaty benefits with respect to a particular item of income under paragraph 3, the resident is entitled to all benefits of the Convention insofar as they affect the taxation of that item of income in the other State. Set forth below is a discussion of each of the three prongs of the test under paragraph 3.

Trade or Business -- Subparagraph 3(a)(i)

The term "trade or business" is not defined in the Convention. Pursuant to paragraph 2 of Article 3 (General Definitions), when determining whether a resident of Slovenia is entitled to the benefits of the Convention under paragraph 3 with respect to income derived from U.S. sources, the United States will ascribe to this term the meaning that it has under the law of the United States. Accordingly, the United States competent authority will refer to the regulations issued under section 367(a) for the definition of the term "trade or business." In general, therefore, a trade or business will be considered to be a specific unified group of activities that constitute or could constitute an independent economic enterprise carried on for profit. Furthermore, a corporation generally will be considered to carry on a trade or business only if the officers and employees of the corporation conduct substantial managerial and operational activities. See, Code section 367(a)(3) and the regulations thereunder.

Subparagraph 3(a)(i) provides that the business of making or managing investments will be considered to be a trade or business only when part of banking, insurance or securities activities conducted by a bank, insurance company, or registered securities dealer. Conversely, such activities conducted by a person other than a bank, insurance company or registered securities dealer will not be considered to be the conduct of an active trade or business, nor would they be considered to be the conduct of an active trade or business if conducted by a bank, insurance company or registered securities dealer but not as part of the company's banking, insurance or dealer business.

Because a headquarters operation is in the business of managing investments, a company that functions solely as a headquarter company will not be considered to be engaged in an active trade or business for purposes of paragraph 3.

Derived in Connection With Requirement - Subparagraphs 3(a)(ii) and (b)

Subparagraph 3(b) provides that income is derived in connection with a trade or business if the income-producing activity in the other State is a line of business that forms a part of or is complementary to the trade or business conducted in the State of residence by the income recipient. Although no definition of the terms "forms a part of" or "complementary" is set forth in the Convention, it is intended that a business activity generally will be considered to "form a part of" a business activity conducted in the other State if the two activities involve the design, manufacture or sale of the same products or type of products, or the provision of similar services. In order for two activities to be considered to be "complementary," the activities need not relate to the same types of products or services, but they should be part of the same overall industry and be related in the sense that the success or failure of one activity will tend to result in success or failure for the other. In cases in which more than one trade or business is conducted in the other State and only one of the trades or businesses forms a part of or is complementary to a trade or business conducted in the State of residence, it is necessary to identify the trade or business to which an item of income is attributable. Royalties generally will be considered to be derived in connection with the trade or business to which the underlying intangible property is attributable. Dividends will be deemed to be derived first out of earnings and profits of the treaty-benefitted trade or business, and then out of other earnings and profits. Interest income may be allocated under any reasonable method consistently applied. A method that conforms to U.S. principles for expense allocation will be considered a reasonable method. The following examples illustrate the application of subparagraph 3(b).

Example 1. USCo is a corporation resident in the United States. USCo is engaged in an active manufacturing business in the United States. USCo owns 100 percent of the shares of

SlovCo, a corporation resident in Slovenia. SlovCo's distributes USCo products in Slovenia. Since the business activities conducted by the two corporations involve the same products, SlovCo's distribution business is considered to form a part of USCo's manufacturing business within the meaning of subparagraph 3(b).

Example 2. The facts are the same as in Example 1, except that USCo does not manufacture. Rather, USCo operates a large research and development facility in the United States that licenses intellectual property to affiliates worldwide, including SlovCo. SlovCo and other USCo affiliates then manufacture and market the USCo-designed products in their respective markets. Since the activities conducted by SlovCo and USCo involve the same product lines, these activities are considered to form a part of the same trade or business.

Example 3. Americair is a corporation resident in the United States that operates an international airline. SlovSub is a wholly-owned subsidiary of Americair resident in Slovenia. SlovSub operates a chain of hotels in Slovenia that are located near airports served by Americair flights. Americair frequently sells tour packages that include air travel to Slovenia and lodging at SlovSub hotels. Although both companies are engaged in the active conduct of a trade or business, the businesses of operating a chain of hotels and operating an airline are distinct trades or businesses. Therefore SlovSub's business does not form a part of Americair's business. However, SlovSub's business is considered to be complementary to Americair's business because they are part of the same overall industry (travel) and the links between their operations tend to make them interdependent.

Example 4. The facts are the same as in Example 3, except that SlovSub owns an office building in Slovenia instead of a hotel chain. No part of Americair's business is conducted through the office building. SlovSub's business is not considered to form a part of or to be complementary to Americair's business. They are engaged in distinct trades or businesses in separate industries, and there is no economic dependence between the two operations.

Example 5. USFlower is a corporation resident in the United States. USFlower produces and sells flowers in the United States and other countries. USFlower owns all the shares of SlovHolding, a corporation resident in Slovenia. SlovHolding is a holding company that is not engaged in a trade or business. SlovHolding owns all the shares of three corporations that are resident in Slovenia: SlovFlower, SlovLawn, and SlovFish. SlovFlower distributes USFlower flowers under the USFlower trademark in Slovenia. SlovLawn markets a line of lawn care products in Slovenia under the USFlower trademark. In addition to being sold under the same trademark, SlovLawn and SlovFlower products are sold in the same stores and sales of each company's products tend to generate increased sales of the other's products. SlovFish imports fish from the United States and distributes it to fish wholesalers in Slovenia. For purposes of paragraph 3, the business of SlovFlower forms a part of the business of USFlower, the business of SlovLawn is complementary to the business of USFlower, and the business of SlovFish is neither part of nor complementary to that of USFlower.

Finally, a resident in one of the States also will be entitled to the benefits of the Convention with respect to income derived from the other State if the income is "incidental" to the trade or business conducted in the recipient's State of residence. Subparagraph 3(b) provides that income derived from a State will be incidental to a trade or business conducted in the other State if the production of such income facilitates the conduct of the trade or business in the other State. An example of incidental income is the temporary investment of working capital derived from a trade or business.

Substantiality -- Subparagraph 3(a)(iii)

As indicated above, subparagraph 3(a)(iii) provides that income that a resident of a State derives from the other State will be entitled to the benefits of the Convention under paragraph 3 only if the income is derived in connection with a trade or business conducted in the recipient's State of residence and that trade or business is "substantial" in relation to the income-producing activity in the other State. Whether the trade or business of the income recipient is substantial will be determined based on all the facts and circumstances. These circumstances generally would include the relative scale of the activities conducted in the two States and the relative contributions made to the conduct of the trade or businesses in the two States.

Paragraph 4

Paragraph 4 provides that a resident of one of the States that is not otherwise entitled to the benefits of the Convention may be granted benefits under the Convention if the competent authority of the State from which benefits are claimed so determines. This discretionary provision is included in recognition of the fact that, with the increasing scope and diversity of international economic relations, there may be cases where significant participation by third country residents in an enterprise of a Contracting State is warranted by sound business practice or long-standing business structures and does not necessarily indicate a motive of attempting to derive unintended Convention benefits.

The competent authority of a State will base a determination under this paragraph on whether the establishment, acquisition, or maintenance of the person seeking benefits under the Convention, or the conduct of such person's operations, has or had as one of its principal purposes the obtaining of benefits under the Convention. Thus, persons that establish operations in one of the States with the principal purpose of obtaining the benefits of the Convention ordinarily will not be granted relief under paragraph 4.

The competent authority may determine to grant all benefits of the Convention, or it may determine to grant only certain benefits. For instance, it may determine to grant benefits only with respect to a particular item of income in a manner similar to paragraph 3. Further, the competent authority may set time limits on the duration of any relief granted.

It is assumed that, for purposes of implementing paragraph 4, a taxpayer will not be required to wait until the tax authorities of one of the States have determined that benefits are denied before he will be permitted to seek a determination under this paragraph. In these circumstances, it is also expected that if the competent authority determines that benefits are to be allowed, they will be allowed retroactively to the time of entry into force of the relevant treaty provision or the establishment of the structure in question, whichever is later.

Finally, there may be cases in which a resident of a Contracting State may apply for discretionary relief to the competent authority of his State of residence. For instance, a resident of a State could apply to the competent authority of his State of residence in a case in which he had been denied a treaty-based credit under Article 23 on the grounds that he was not entitled to benefits of the article under Article 22.

Paragraph 5

Paragraph 5 provides that the term "recognized stock exchange" means (a) the NASDAQ System owned by the National Association of Securities Dealers, and any stock exchange registered with the Securities and Exchange Commission as a national securities exchange for purposes of the Securities Exchange Act of 1934, (b) the Ljubljana Stock Exchange, and (c) the stock exchanges of Frankfurt, London, Paris and Vienna. In addition, subparagraph (c) of paragraph 5 provides for the competent authorities to agree upon any other stock exchanges.

ARTICLE 23 (RELIEF FROM DOUBLE TAXATION)

This Article describes the manner in which each Contracting State undertakes to relieve double taxation. The United States uses the foreign tax credit method under its internal law, and by treaty.

Paragraph 1

The United States agrees, in paragraph 1, to allow to its citizens and residents a credit against U.S. tax for income taxes paid or accrued to Slovenia. Paragraph 1 also provides that Slovenia's covered taxes (other than the assets tax on banks and savings institutions) are income taxes for U.S. purposes. This provision is based on the Treasury Department's review of Slovenia's laws.

The credit under the Convention is allowed in accordance with the provisions and subject to the limitations of U.S. law, as that law may be amended over time, so long as the general principle of this Article, i.e., the allowance of a credit, is retained. Thus, although the Convention provides for a foreign tax credit, the terms of the credit are determined by the provisions, at the time a credit is given, of the U.S. statutory credit.

As indicated, the U.S. credit under the Convention is subject to the various limitations of U.S. law (see Code sections 901 - 908). For example, the credit against U.S. tax generally is limited to the amount of U.S. tax due with respect to net foreign source income within the relevant foreign tax credit limitation category (see Code section 904(a) and (d)), and the dollar amount of the credit is determined in accordance with U.S. currency translation rules (see, e.g., Code section 986). Similarly, U.S. law applies to determine carryover periods for excess credits and other inter-year adjustments. When the alternative minimum tax is due, the alternative minimum tax foreign tax credit generally is limited in accordance with U.S. law to 90 percent of alternative minimum tax liability. Furthermore, nothing in the Convention prevents the limitation of the U.S. credit from being applied on a per-country basis (should internal law be changed), an overall basis, or to particular categories of income (see, e.g., Code section 865(h)).

Subparagraph (b) provides for a deemed-paid credit, consistent with section 902 of the Code, to a U.S. corporation in respect of dividends received from a corporation resident in Slovenia of which the U.S. corporation owns at least 10 percent of the voting stock. This credit is for the tax paid by the corporation of Slovenia on the profits out of which the dividends are considered paid.

Paragraph 2

Paragraph 2 contains the rules under which Slovenia will avoid double taxation under the Convention. It follows Article 23B (Credit Method) of the OECD Model. Under this paragraph, Slovenia agrees to allow a credit to a resident of Slovenia deriving income from the United States for United States tax paid (as defined in subparagraph 1(a) and 2 of Article 2 (Taxes Covered)), to the extent it is paid in accordance with the Convention. The credit is for the full amount of United States tax, but not to exceed the Slovenian tax on that income.

Paragraph 3

Paragraph 3 provides special rules for the tax treatment in both States of certain types of income derived from U.S. sources by U.S. citizens who are resident in Slovenia. Since U.S. citizens, regardless of residence, are subject to United States tax at ordinary progressive rates on their worldwide income, the U.S. tax on the U.S. source income of a U.S. citizen resident in Slovenia may exceed the U.S. tax that may be imposed under the Convention on an item of U.S. source income derived by a resident of Slovenia who is not a U.S. citizen.

Subparagraph (a) of paragraph 3 provides special credit rules for Slovenia with respect to items of income that are either exempt from U.S. tax or subject to reduced rates of U.S. tax under the provisions of the Convention when received by residents of Slovenia who are not U.S. citizens. The tax credit of Slovenia allowed by paragraph 3(a) under these circumstances, to the extent consistent with the law of Slovenia, need not exceed the U.S. tax that may be imposed under the provisions of the Convention, other than tax imposed solely by reason of the U.S. citizenship of the taxpayer under the provisions of the saving clause of paragraph 4 of Article 1 (General Scope). Thus, if a U.S. citizen resident in Slovenia receives U.S. source contingent interest, the foreign tax credit granted by Slovenia would be limited to 15 percent of the interest -- the U.S. tax that may be imposed under subparagraph 8(a) of Article 11 (Interest) -- even if the shareholder is subject to U.S. net income tax because of his U.S. citizenship.

Paragraph 3(b) eliminates the potential for double taxation that can arise because subparagraph 3(a) provides that Slovenia need not provide full relief for the U.S. tax imposed on its citizens resident in Slovenia. The subparagraph provides that the United States will credit the income tax paid or accrued to Slovenia, after the application of subparagraph 3(a). It further provides that in allowing the credit, the United States will not reduce its tax below the amount that is taken into account in Slovenia in applying subparagraph 3(a). Since the income described in paragraph 3 is U.S. source income, special rules are required to resource some of the income to Slovenia in order for the United States to be able to credit Slovenia's tax. This resourcing is provided for in subparagraph 3(c), which deems the items of income referred to in subparagraph 3(a) to be from foreign sources to the extent necessary to avoid double taxation under paragraph 3(b). The rules of paragraph 3(c) apply only for purposes of determining U.S. foreign tax credits with respect to taxes referred to in paragraphs 2(b) and 3 of Article 2 (Taxes Covered).

The following two examples illustrate the application of paragraph 3 in the case of a U.S. source contingent interest received by a U.S. citizen resident in Slovenia. In both examples, the U.S. rate of tax on residents of Slovenia under subparagraph 8(a) of Article 11 (Interest) of the Convention is 15 percent. In both examples the U.S. income tax rate on the U.S. citizen is 36 percent. In example I, the income tax rate on its resident (the U.S. citizen) is 25 percent (below the U.S. rate), and in example II, the rate on its resident is 40 percent (above the U.S. rate).

	Example I	Example II
Paragraph 3(a)		
U.S. contingent interest	$100.00	$100.00
Notional U.S. withholding tax per Article 11(8)(a)	15.00	15.00
Slovenia taxable income	100.00	100.00
Slovenia tax before credit	25.00	40.00
Slovenia foreign tax credit	15.00	15.00
Net post-credit Slovenian tax	10.00	25.00
Paragraphs 3(b) and (c)		
U.S. pre-tax income	$100.00	$100.00
U.S. pre-credit citizenship tax	36.00	36.00
Notional U.S. withholding tax	15.00	15.00
U.S. tax available for credit	21.00	21.00
Income resourced from U.S. to Slovenia	27.77	58.33
U.S. tax on resourced income	10.00	21.00
U.S. credit for other State tax	10.00	21.00
Net post-credit U.S. tax	11.00	0.00
Total U.S. tax	26.00	15.00

In both examples, in the application of paragraph 3(a), Slovenia credits a 15 percent U.S. tax against its residence tax on the U.S. citizen. In example I, the net Slovenian tax after foreign tax credit is $10.00; in the second example it is $25.00. In the application of paragraphs 3(b) and (c), from the U.S. tax due before credit of $36.00, the United States subtracts the amount of the U.S. source tax of $15.00, against which no U.S. foreign tax credit is to be allowed. This provision assures that the United States will collect the tax that it is due under the Convention as the source country. In both examples, the maximum amount of U.S. tax against which credit for Slovenian tax may be claimed is $21.00. Initially, all of the income in these examples was U.S. source. In order for a U.S. credit to be allowed for the full amount of the Slovenian tax, an appropriate amount of the income must be resourced. The amount that must be resourced depends on the amount of Slovenian tax for which the U.S. citizen is claiming a U.S. foreign tax credit. In example I, the Slovenian tax was $10.00. In order for this amount to be creditable against U.S. tax, $27.77 ($10 divided by .36) must be resourced as foreign source. When Slovenian tax is credited against the U.S. tax on the resourced income, there is a net U.S. tax of $11.00 due after credit. In example II, Slovenian tax was $25 but, because the amount available for credit is reduced under subparagraph 3(c) by the amount of the U.S. source tax, only $21.00 is eligible for credit. Accordingly, the amount that must be resourced is limited to the amount necessary to ensure a foreign tax credit for $21 of other State tax, or $58.33 ($21 divided by .36). Thus, even though Slovenian tax was $25.00 and the U.S. tax available for credit was $21.00, there is no excess credit available for carryover.

Paragraph 4

Paragraph 4 provides that where income derived by a resident of a Contracting State is exempt from tax in that State, the Contracting State may, in determining the tax on the remaining income of the resident, apply the rate of tax as if the exempted income had not been exempt (ie, exemption with progression).

Relation to other articles

By virtue of the exceptions in subparagraph 5(a) of Article 1, this Article is not subject to the saving clause of paragraph 4 of Article 1 (General Scope). Thus, the United States will allow a credit to its citizens and residents in accordance with the Article, even if such credit were to provide a benefit not available under the Code (such as the re-sourcing provided by subparagraph 3(c)).

ARTICLE 24 (NON-DISCRIMINATION)

This Article assures that nationals of a Contracting State, in the case of paragraph 1, and residents of a Contracting State, in the case of paragraphs 2 through 4, will not be subject, directly or indirectly, to discriminatory taxation in the other Contracting State. For this purpose, non-discrimination means providing national treatment. Not all differences in tax treatment, either as between nationals of the two States, or between residents of the two States, are violations of this national treatment standard. Rather, the national treatment obligation of this Article applies only if the nationals or residents of the two States are comparably situated.

Each of the relevant paragraphs of the Article provides that two persons that are comparably situated must be treated similarly. Although the actual words differ from paragraph to paragraph (e.g., paragraph 1 refers to two nationals "in the same circumstances," paragraph 2 refers to two enterprises "carrying on the same activities" and paragraph 4 refers to two enterprises that are "similar"), the common underlying premise is that if the difference in treatment is directly related to a tax-relevant difference in the situations of the domestic and foreign persons being compared, that difference is not to be treated as discriminatory (e.g., if one person is taxable in a Contracting State on worldwide income and the other is not, or tax may be collectible from one person at a later stage, but not from the other, distinctions in treatment would be justified under paragraph 1). Other examples of such factors that can lead to non-discriminatory differences in treatment will be noted in the discussions of each paragraph.

The operative paragraphs of the Article also use different language to identify the kinds of differences in taxation treatment that will be considered discriminatory. For example, paragraphs 1 and 4 speak of "any taxation or any requirement connected therewith that is more burdensome," while paragraph 2 specifies that a tax "shall not be less favorably levied." Regardless of these differences in language, only differences in tax treatment that materially disadvantage the foreign person relative to the domestic person are properly the subject of the Article.

Paragraph 1

Paragraph 1 provides that a national of one Contracting State may not be subject to taxation or connected requirements in the other Contracting State that are more burdensome than the taxes and connected requirements imposed upon a national of that other State in the same circumstances. The OECD Model prohibits taxation that is "other than or more burdensome" than that imposed on U.S. persons. This Convention, consistent with the U.S. Model, omits the reference to taxation that is "other than" that imposed on U.S. persons because the only relevant question under this provision should be whether the requirement imposed on a national of Slovenia is more burdensome. A requirement may be different from the requirements imposed on U.S. nationals without being more burdensome.

As noted above, whether or not the two persons are both taxable on worldwide income is a significant circumstance for this purpose. The 1992 revision of the OECD Model added after the words "in the same circumstances", the phrase "in particular with respect to residence," reflecting the fact that under most countries' laws residents are taxable on worldwide income and nonresidents are not.

Because the relevant circumstances referred to relate, among other things, to taxation on worldwide income, paragraph 1 does not obligate the United States to apply the same taxing regime to a national of Slovenia who is not resident in the United States and a U.S. national who is not resident in the United States. United States citizens who are not residents of the United

States but who are, nevertheless, subject to United States tax on their worldwide income are not in the same circumstances with respect to United States taxation as citizens of Slovenia who are not United States residents. To reflect the difference in the basis of taxation between the U.S. and other systems, the Convention states explicitly that U.S. citizens who are not residents of the United States but who are, nevertheless, subject to U.S. tax on their worldwide income, are not in the same circumstances with respect to U.S. taxation as nationals of Slovenia who are not U.S. residents. The underlying concept is essentially the same in the OECD Model, the U.S. Model, and the Convention.

A national of a Contracting State is afforded protection under this paragraph even if the national is not a resident of either Contracting State. Thus, a U.S. citizen who is resident in a third country is entitled, under this paragraph, to the same treatment in Slovenia as a national of Slovenia who is in similar circumstances (i.e., presumably one who is resident in a third State). The term "national" in relation to a Contracting State is defined in subparagraph 1(h) of Article 3 (General Definitions). The term includes both individuals and juridical persons.

Paragraph 2

Paragraph 2 of the Article, like the comparable paragraphs in the OECD and U.S. Models, provides that a Contracting State may not tax a permanent establishment or fixed base of a resident or an enterprise of the other Contracting State less favorably than a resident or an enterprise of that first-mentioned State that is carrying on the same activities. This provision, however, does not obligate a Contracting State to grant to a resident of the other Contracting State any tax allowances, reliefs, etc., that it grants to its own residents on account of their civil status or family responsibilities. Thus, if a sole proprietor who is a resident of Slovenia has a permanent establishment in the United States, in assessing income tax on the profits attributable to the permanent establishment, the United States is not obligated to allow to the resident of Slovenia the personal allowances for himself and his family that he would be permitted to take if the permanent establishment were a sole proprietorship owned and operated by a U.S. resident, despite the fact that the individual income tax rates would apply.

The fact that a U.S. permanent establishment of an enterprise of Slovenia is subject to U.S. tax only on income that is attributable to the permanent establishment, while a U.S. corporation engaged in the same activities is taxable on its worldwide income is not, in itself, a sufficient difference to deny national treatment to the permanent establishment. There are cases, however, where the two enterprises would not be similarly situated and differences in treatment may be warranted. For instance, it would not be a violation of the non-discrimination protection of paragraph 2 to require the foreign enterprise to provide information in a reasonable manner that may be different from the information requirements imposed on a resident enterprise, because information may not be as readily available to the Internal Revenue Service from a foreign as from a domestic enterprise. Similarly, it would not be a violation of paragraph 2 to impose penalties on persons who fail to comply with such a requirement (see, e.g., sections 874(a) and 882(c)(2)). Further, a determination that income and expenses have been attributed or allocated to a permanent establishment in conformity with the principles of Article 7 (Business Profits) implies that the attribution or allocation was not discriminatory.

Section 1446 of the Code imposes on any partnership with income that is effectively connected with a U.S. trade or business the obligation to withhold tax on amounts allocable to a foreign partner. In the context of the Convention, this obligation applies with respect to a share of the partnership income of a partner resident in Slovenia, and attributable to a U.S. permanent establishment. There is no similar obligation with respect to the distributive shares of U.S. resident partners. It is understood, however, that this distinction is not a form of discrimination within the meaning of paragraph 2 of the Article. No distinction is made between U.S. and non-U.S. partnerships, since the law requires that partnerships of both U.S. and non-U.S. domicile withhold tax in respect of the partnership shares of non-U.S. partners. Furthermore, in distinguishing between U.S. and non-U.S. partners, the requirement to withhold on the non-U.S. but not the U.S. partner's share is not discriminatory taxation, but, like other withholding on nonresident aliens, is merely a reasonable method for the collection of tax from persons who are not continually present in the United States, and as to whom it otherwise may be difficult for the United States to enforce its tax jurisdiction. If tax has been over-withheld, the partner can, as in other cases of over-withholding, file for a refund. (The relationship between paragraph 2 and the imposition of the branch tax is dealt with below in the discussion of paragraph 5.)

Paragraph 2 obligates the host State to provide national treatment not only to permanent establishments of an enterprise of the other Contracting State, but also to other residents of that State that are taxable in the host State on a net basis because they derive income from independent personal services performed in the host State that is attributable to a fixed base in that State. Thus, an individual resident of Slovenia who performs independent personal services in the United States, and who is subject to U.S. income tax on the income from those services that is attributable to a fixed base in the United States, is entitled to no less favorable tax treatment in the United States than a U.S. resident engaged in the same kinds of activities. With such a rule in a treaty, the host State cannot tax its own residents on a net basis, but disallow deductions (other than personal allowances, etc.) with respect to the income attributable to the fixed base. Similarly, in accordance with paragraph 5 of Article 6 (Income from Real Property (Immovable Property)), the situs State would be required to allow deductions to a resident of the other State with respect to income derived from real property located in the situs State to the same extent that deductions are allowed to residents of the situs State with respect to income derived from real property located in the situs State.

Paragraph 3

Paragraph 3 prohibits discrimination in the allowance of deductions. When a resident or an enterprise of a Contracting State pays interest, royalties or other disbursements to a resident of the other Contracting State, the first-mentioned Contracting State must allow a deduction for those payments in computing the taxable profits of the resident or enterprise as if the payment had been made under the same conditions to a resident of the first-mentioned Contracting State. An exception to this rule is provided for cases where the provisions of paragraph 1 of Article 9

(Associated Enterprises), paragraph 7 of Article 11 (Interest) or paragraph 6 of Article 12 (Royalties) apply, because in these situations, the related parties have entered into transactions on an arm's length basis. This exception would include the denial or deferral of certain interest deductions under Code section 163(j).

The term "other disbursements" is understood to include a reasonable allocation of executive and general administrative expenses, research and development expenses and other expenses incurred for the benefit of a group of related persons that includes the person incurring the expense.

Paragraph 3 also provides that any debts of a resident or an enterprise of a Contracting State to a resident of the other Contracting State are deductible in the first-mentioned Contracting State for computing the capital tax of the enterprise under the same conditions as if the debt had been contracted to a resident of the first-mentioned Contracting State. Even though, for general purposes, the only capital tax covered by the Convention is Slovenia's business assets tax, under paragraph 6 of this Article, the non-discrimination provisions apply to all taxes levied in both Contracting States, at all levels of government. Thus, this provision may be relevant for both States, as many local governments in the United States impose capital taxes.

Paragraph 4

Paragraph 4 requires that a Contracting State not impose more burdensome taxation or connected requirements on an enterprise of that State that is wholly or partly owned or controlled, directly or indirectly, by one or more residents of the other Contracting State, than the taxation or connected requirements that it imposes on other similar enterprises of that first-mentioned Contracting State. For this purpose it is understood that "similar" refers to similar activities or ownership of the enterprise.

This rule, like all non-discrimination provisions, does not prohibit differing treatment of entities that are in differing circumstances. Rather, a protected enterprise is only required to be treated in the same manner as other enterprises that, from the point of view of the application of the tax law, are in substantially similar circumstances both in law and in fact. The taxation of a distributing corporation under section 367(e) on an applicable distribution to foreign shareholders does not violate paragraph 4 of the Article because a foreign-owned corporation is not similar to a domestically-owned corporation that is accorded nonrecognition treatment under sections 337 and 355.

For the reasons given above in connection with the discussion of paragraph 2 of the Article, it is also understood that the provision in section 1446 of the Code for withholding of tax on non-U.S. partners does not violate paragraph 4 of the Article.

It is further understood that the ineligibility of a U.S. corporation with nonresident alien shareholders to make an election to be an "S" corporation does not violate paragraph 4 of the Article. If a corporation elects to be an S corporation (requiring 75 or fewer shareholders), it is generally not subject to income tax and the shareholders take into account their pro rata shares of the corporation's items of income, loss, deduction or credit. (The purpose of the provision is to allow an individual or small group of individuals to conduct business in corporate form while paying taxes at individual rates as if the business were conducted directly.) A nonresident alien does not pay U.S. tax on a net basis, and, thus, does not generally take into account items of loss, deduction or credit. Thus, the S corporation provisions do not exclude corporations with nonresident alien shareholders because such shareholders are foreign, but only because they are not net-basis taxpayers. Similarly, the provisions exclude corporations with other types of shareholders where the purpose of the provisions cannot be fulfilled or their mechanics implemented. For example, corporations with corporate shareholders are excluded because the purpose of the provision to permit individuals to conduct a business in corporate form at individual tax rates would not be furthered by their inclusion.

Paragraph 5

Paragraph 5 of the Article confirms that no provision of the Article will prevent either Contracting State from imposing the branch taxes described in paragraph 8 of Article 10 (Dividends) and paragraph 9 of Article 11 (Interest). Since imposition of the branch taxes under the Convention is specifically sanctioned by paragraph 8 of Article 10 (Dividends) and paragraph 9 of Article 11 (Interest), imposition of these taxes could not be precluded by Article 24, even without paragraph 5. Under the generally accepted rule of construction that the specific takes precedence over the more general, the specific branch tax provisions of Article 10 and Article 11 would take precedence over the more general national treatment provision of Article 24.

Paragraph 6

As noted above, notwithstanding the specification in Article 2 (Taxes Covered) of taxes covered by the Convention for general purposes, for purposes of providing non-discrimination protection this Article applies to taxes of every kind and description imposed by a Contracting State or a political subdivision or local authority thereof. Customs duties are not considered to be taxes for this purpose.

Relation to Other Articles

The saving clause of paragraph 4 of Article 1 (General Scope) does not apply to this Article, by virtue of the exceptions in paragraph 5(a) of Article 1. Thus, for example, a U.S. citizen who is a resident of Slovenia may claim benefits in the United States under this Article.

Nationals of a Contracting State may claim the benefits of paragraph 1 regardless of whether they are entitled to benefits under Article 22 (Limitation on Benefits), because that paragraph applies to nationals and not residents. They may not claim the benefits of the other paragraphs of this Article with respect to an item of income unless they are generally entitled to treaty benefits with respect to that income under a provision of Article 22.

ARTICLE 25 (MUTUAL AGREEMENT PROCEDURE)

This Article provides the mechanism for taxpayers to bring to the attention of the Contracting States' competent authorities issues and problems that may arise under the Convention. It also provides a mechanism for cooperation between the competent authorities of the Contracting States to resolve disputes and clarify issues that may arise under the Convention and to resolve cases of double taxation not provided for in the Convention. The competent authorities of the two Contracting States are identified in paragraph 1(e) of Article 3 (General Definitions).

Paragraph 1

This paragraph provides that where a resident of a Contracting State considers that the actions of one or both Contracting States will result in taxation that is not in accordance with the Convention he may present his case to the competent authority of the Contracting State of which he is a resident, or if his case comes under paragraph 1 of Article 24 (Non-Discrimination), to the Contracting State of which he is a national.

Although the typical cases brought under this paragraph will involve economic double taxation arising from transfer pricing adjustments, the scope of this paragraph is not limited to such cases. For example, if the United States treats income derived by a company resident in Slovenia as attributable to a permanent establishment in the United States, and the Slovenian resident believes that the income is not attributable to a permanent establishment, or that no permanent establishment exists, the Slovenian resident may bring a complaint under paragraph 1 to the competent authority of Slovenia.

It is not necessary for a person bringing a complaint first to have exhausted the remedies provided under the national laws of the Contracting States before presenting a case to the competent authorities. Unlike the U.S. Model, but like the OECD Model, paragraph 1 provides that a case must be presented to a competent authority within a specified period (in this Convention, five years, in the OECD Model, three years) from first notification of the action giving rise to taxation not in accordance with the provisions of the Convention. Paragraph 18 of the Commentaries to the OECD Model states that identifying the date of the first notification, as referred to in paragraph 1, should be done in the manner most favorable to the taxpayer. For example, if an action results from the tax authority following a published procedure, the first notification would not be the date of publication of the procedure, but rather the date on which the taxpayer was first notified of the decision to apply the procedure to him.

Paragraph 2

This paragraph instructs the competent authorities in dealing with cases brought by taxpayers under paragraph 1. It provides that if the competent authority of the Contracting State to which the case is presented judges the case to have merit, and cannot reach a unilateral solution, it shall seek an agreement with the competent authority of the other Contracting State pursuant to which taxation not in accordance with the Convention will be avoided. During the period that a proceeding under this Article is pending, any assessment and collection procedures shall be suspended. Any agreement is to be implemented even if such implementation otherwise would be barred by the statute of limitations or by some other procedural limitation, such as a closing agreement. In a case where the taxpayer has entered a closing agreement (or other written settlement) with the United States prior to bringing a case to the competent authorities, the U.S. competent authority will endeavor only to obtain a correlative adjustment from Slovenia. See, Rev. Proc. 96-13, 1996-3 I.R.B. 31, section 7.05. Because, as specified in paragraph 2 of Article 1 (General Scope), the Convention cannot operate to increase a taxpayer's liability, time or other procedural limitations can be overridden only for the purpose of making refunds and not to impose additional tax.

Paragraph 3

Paragraph 3 authorizes the competent authorities to resolve difficulties or doubts that may arise as to the application or interpretation of the Convention. The paragraph includes a non-exhaustive list of examples of the kinds of matters about which the competent authorities may reach agreement. This list is purely illustrative; it does not grant any authority that is not implicitly present as a result of the introductory sentence of paragraph 3. The competent authorities may, for example, agree to the same attribution of income, deductions, credits or allowances between an enterprise in one Contracting State and its permanent establishment in the other (subparagraph (a)) or between related persons (subparagraph (b)). These allocations are to be made in accordance with the arm's length principle underlying Article 7 (Business Profits) and Article 9 (Associated Enterprises). Agreements reached under these subparagraphs may include agreement on a methodology for determining an appropriate transfer price, common treatment of a taxpayer's cost sharing arrangement, or upon an acceptable range of results under that methodology.

As indicated in subparagraphs (c), (d), (e) and (f), the competent authorities also may agree to settle a variety of conflicting applications of the Convention. They may agree to characterize particular items of income in the same way (subparagraph (c)), to characterize entities in a particular way (subparagraph (d)), to apply the same source rules to particular items of income (subparagraph (e)), and to adopt a common meaning of a term (subparagraph f)).

Subparagraph (g) makes clear that the competent authorities can agree that the conditions for application of the anti-abuse provisions in paragraph 10 of Article 10 (Dividends), paragraph 10 of Article 11 (Interest), paragraph 7 of Article 12 (Royalties), or paragraph 3 of Article 21 (Other Income) have been met. As with all other matters, the competent authorities' agreement does not have to relate to a particular case. Thus, if the competent authorities become aware of a type of transaction entered into by several taxpayers, they could reach an agreement that all such transactions are entered into with a main purpose of taking advantage of a relevant Article. In that case, treaty benefits would be denied to all taxpayers who had entered into such transactions. It is anticipated that the public would be notified of such generic agreements through the issuance of press releases. It is anticipated that the standard of judicial review regarding such an agreement would be the same as for a determination with respect to a particular taxpayer.

Since the list under paragraph 3 is not exhaustive, the competent authorities may reach agreement on issues not enumerated in paragraph 3 if necessary to avoid double taxation. For example, the competent authorities may seek agreement on a uniform set of standards for the use of exchange rates, or agree on consistent timing of gain recognition with respect to a transaction to the extent necessary to avoid double taxation. Agreements reached by the competent authorities under paragraph 3 need not conform to the internal law provisions of either Contracting State.

Finally, paragraph 3 authorizes the competent authorities to consult for the purpose of eliminating double taxation in cases not provided for in the Convention and to resolve any difficulties or doubts arising as to the interpretation or application of the Convention. This provision is intended to permit the competent authorities to implement the treaty in particular cases in a manner that is consistent with its expressed general purposes. It permits the competent authorities to deal with cases that are within the spirit of the provisions but that are not specifically covered. An example of such a case might be double taxation arising from a transfer pricing adjustment between two permanent establishments of a third-country resident, one in the United States and one in Slovenia. Since no resident of a Contracting State is involved in the case, the Convention does not apply, but the competent authorities nevertheless may use the authority of the Convention to prevent the double taxation.

Paragraph 4

Paragraph 4 authorizes the competent authorities to increase any dollar amounts referred to in the Convention to reflect economic and monetary developments. Under the Convention, this refers to Articles 17 (Artistes and Sportsmen) and Article 20 (Students, Trainees, Professors and Researchers). The rule under paragraph 4 is intended to operate as follows: if, for example, after the Convention has been in force for some time, inflation rates have been such as to make the $15,000 exemption threshold for entertainers in Article 17 (Artistes and Sportsmen) unrealistically low in terms of the original objectives intended in setting the threshold, the competent authorities may agree to a higher threshold without the need for formal amendment to the treaty and ratification by the Contracting States. This authority can be exercised, however, only to the extent necessary to restore those original objectives. This provision can be applied only to the benefit of taxpayers, i.e., only to increase thresholds, not to reduce them.

Paragraph 5

Paragraph 5 provides that the competent authorities may communicate with each other for the purpose of reaching an agreement. This makes clear that the competent authorities of the two Contracting States may communicate without going through diplomatic channels. Such communication may be in various forms, including, where appropriate, through face-to-face meetings of the competent authorities or their representatives.

Other Issues

Treaty effective dates and termination in relation to competent authority dispute resolution

A case may be raised by a taxpayer under a treaty with respect to a year for which a treaty was in force after the treaty has been terminated. In such a case the ability of the competent authorities to act is limited. They may not exchange confidential information, nor may they reach a solution that varies from that specified in its law.

A case also may be brought to a competent authority under a treaty that is in force, but with respect to a year prior to the entry into force of the treaty. The scope of the competent authorities to address such a case is not constrained by the fact that the treaty was not in force when the transactions at issue occurred, and the competent authorities have available to them the full range of remedies afforded under this Article.

Triangular competent authority solutions

International tax cases may involve more than two taxing jurisdictions (e.g., transactions among a parent corporation resident in country A and its subsidiaries resident in countries B and C). As long as there is a complete network of treaties among the three countries, it should be possible, under the full combination of bilateral authorities, for the competent authorities of the three States to work together on a three-sided solution. Although country A may not be able to give information received under Article 26 (Exchange of Information and Administrative Assistance) from country B to the authorities of country C, if the competent authorities of the three countries are working together, it should not be a problem for them to arrange for the authorities of country B to give the necessary information directly to the tax authorities of country C, as well as to those of country A. Each bilateral part of the trilateral solution must, of course, not exceed the scope of the authority of the competent authorities under the relevant bilateral treaty.

Relation to Other Articles

This Article is not subject to the saving clause of paragraph 4 of Article 1 (General Scope) by virtue of the exceptions in paragraph 5(a) of that Article. Thus, rules, definitions, procedures, etc. that are agreed upon by the competent authorities under this Article may be applied by the United States with respect to its citizens and residents even if they differ from the comparable Code provisions. Similarly, as indicated above, U.S. law may be overridden to provide refunds of tax to a U.S. citizen or resident under this Article. A person may seek relief under Article 25 regardless of whether he is generally entitled to benefits under Article 22 (Limitation on Benefits). As in all other cases, the competent authority is vested with the discretion to decide whether the claim for relief is justified.

ARTICLE 26 (EXCHANGE OF INFORMATION AND ADMINISTRATIVE ASSISTANCE)

Paragraph 1

This Article provides for the exchange of information between the competent authorities of the Contracting States. The information to be exchanged is that which is relevant for carrying out the provisions of the Convention or the domestic laws of the United States or of Slovenia concerning the taxes covered by the Convention.

The taxes covered by the Convention for purposes of this Article constitute a broader category of taxes than those referred to in Article 2 (Taxes Covered). As provided in paragraph 4, for purposes of exchange of information, covered taxes include all taxes imposed by the Contracting States. Exchange of information with respect to domestic law is authorized insofar as the taxation under those domestic laws is not contrary to the Convention. Thus, for example, information may be exchanged with respect to a covered tax, even if the transaction to which the information relates is a purely domestic transaction in the requesting State and, therefore, the exchange is not made for the purpose of carrying out the Convention.

An example of such a case is provided in the OECD Commentary: A company resident in the United States and a company resident in Slovenia transact business between themselves through a third-country resident company. Neither Contracting State has a treaty with the third State. In order to enforce their internal laws with respect to transactions of their residents with the third-country company (since there is no relevant treaty in force), the Contracting States may exchange information regarding the prices that their residents paid in their transactions with the third-country resident.

Paragraph 1 states that information exchange is not restricted by Article 1 (General Scope). Accordingly, information may be requested and provided under this Article with respect to persons who are not residents of either Contracting State. For example, if a third-country resident has a permanent establishment in Slovenia which engages in transactions with a U.S. enterprise, the United States could request information with respect to that permanent establishment, even though it is not a resident of either Contracting State. Similarly, if a third--country resident maintains a bank account in Slovenia, and the Internal Revenue Service has reason to believe that funds in that account should have been reported for U.S. tax purposes but have not been so reported, information can be requested from Slovenia with respect to that person's account.

Paragraph 1 also provides assurances that any information exchanged will be treated as secret, subject to the same disclosure constraints as information obtained under the laws of the requesting State. Information received may be disclosed only to persons, including courts and administrative bodies, involved with the assessment, collection, enforcement or prosecution in respect of the taxes to which the information relates, or to persons involved with the administration of these taxes or with the oversight of such activities. The information must be used by these persons in connection with these designated functions. Persons in the United States involved with the oversight of the administration of taxes include legislative bodies, such as the tax-writing committees of Congress and the General Accounting Office. Information received by these bodies must be for use in the performance of their role in overseeing the administration of U.S. tax laws. Information received may be disclosed in public court proceedings or in judicial decisions.

The Article authorizes the competent authorities to exchange information on a routine basis, on request in relation to a specific case, or spontaneously. It is contemplated that the Contracting States will utilize this authority to engage in all of these forms of information exchange, as appropriate.

Paragraph 2

Paragraph 2 provides that the obligations undertaken in paragraph 1 to exchange information do not require a Contracting State to carry out administrative measures that are at variance with the laws or administrative practice of either State. Nor is a Contracting State required to supply information not obtainable under the laws or administrative practice of either State, or to disclose trade secrets or other information, the disclosure of which would be contrary to public policy. Thus, a requesting State may be denied information from the other State if the information would be obtained pursuant to procedures or measures that are broader than those available in the requesting State.

While paragraph 2 states conditions under which a Contracting State is not obligated to comply with a request from the other Contracting State for information, the requested State is not precluded from providing such information, and may, at its discretion, do so subject to the limitations of its internal law.

Paragraph 3

Paragraph 3 sets forth exceptions from the dispensations described in paragraph 2. It provides that when information is requested by a Contracting State in accordance with this Article, the other Contracting State is obligated to obtain the requested information as if the tax in question were the tax of the requested State, even if that State has no direct tax interest in the case to which the request relates.

Paragraph 3 further provides that the requesting State may specify the form in which information is to be provided (e.g., depositions of witnesses and authenticated copies of original documents) so that the information is usable in the judicial proceedings of the requesting State. The requested State should, if possible, provide the information in the form requested to the same extent that it can obtain information in that form under its own laws and administrative practices with respect to its own taxes.

Paragraph 3 omits the first sentence of the comparable paragraph in the U.S. Model which provides that information must be provided to the requesting State notwithstanding the fact that disclosure of the information is precluded by bank secrecy or similar legislation relating to disclosure of financial information by financial institutions or intermediaries. The United States has received assurances from the Slovenian Ministry of Finance concerning Slovenia's ability to exchange third-party information obtained from banks and other financial institutions (hereinafter referred as "banks"). Specifically, Article 30 of Slovenia's Law on Tax procedures allows Slovenia to obtain from banks any and all information relevant to assessment and collection of taxes, whether the information pertains to the party under investigations or another party involved in the tax matter. Article 26 of this law also imposes on banks and savings banks an obligation to send without specific request to the tax authorities information about accounts which are held by individuals and legal persons and information about transactions through these accounts. Accordingly, the Treasury Department believes that the omission of the sentence will not affect the United States' ability to obtain this third-party information from Slovenia.

Paragraph 4

As noted above in the discussion of paragraph 1, the exchange of information provisions of the Convention apply to all taxes imposed by a Contracting State, not just to those taxes designated as covered taxes under Article 2 (Taxes Covered). The U.S. competent authority may, therefore, request information for purposes of, for example, estate and gift taxes or federal excise taxes.

Treaty effective dates and termination in relation to exchange of information

A tax administration may seek information with respect to a year for which a treaty was in force after the treaty has been terminated. In such a case the ability of the other tax administration to act is limited. The treaty no longer provides authority for the tax administrations to exchange confidential information. They may only exchange information pursuant to domestic law.

The competent authority also may seek information under a treaty that is in force, but with respect to a year prior to the entry into force of the treaty. The scope of the competent authorities to address such a case is not constrained by the fact that a treaty was not in force when the transactions at issue occurred, and the competent authorities have available to them the full range of information exchange provisions afforded under this Article. Even though a prior treaty may have been in effect during the years in which the transaction at issue occurred, the exchange of information provisions of the current treaty apply.

ARTICLE 27 (DIPLOMATIC AGENTS AND CONSULAR OFFICERS)

This Article confirms that any fiscal privileges to which diplomatic or consular officials are entitled under general provisions of international law or under special agreements will apply notwithstanding any provisions to the contrary in the Convention. The agreements referred to include any bilateral agreements, such as consular conventions, that affect the taxation of diplomats and consular officials and any multilateral agreements dealing with these issues, such as the Vienna Convention on Diplomatic Relations and the Vienna Convention on Consular Relations. The U.S. generally adheres to the latter because its terms are consistent with customary international law.

The Article does not independently provide any benefits to diplomatic agents and consular officers. Article 19 (Government Service) does so, as do Code section 893 and a number of bilateral and multilateral agreements. In the event that there is a conflict between the tax treaty and international law or such other treaties, under which the diplomatic agent or consular official is entitled to greater benefits under the latter, the latter laws or agreements shall have precedence. Conversely, if the tax treaty confers a greater benefit than another agreement, the affected person could claim the benefit of the tax treaty.

Pursuant to subparagraph 5(b) of Article 1, the saving clause of paragraph 4 of Article 1 (General Scope) does not apply to override any benefits of this Article available to an individual who is neither a citizen of the United States nor has immigrant status in the United States.

ARTICLE 28 (CAPITAL)

This Article specifies the circumstances in which a Contracting State may impose tax on capital owned by a resident of the other Contracting State. While absent from the U.S. Model, the inclusion of a Capital Article is appropriate because of Slovenia's assets tax on banks and savings institutions (the "Assets Tax"). The Assets Tax is a covered tax for Slovenia under subparagraph 1(b) of Article 2 (Taxes Covered). However, it should be noted that in accordance with paragraph 1 of Article 23 (Relief from Double Taxation) the Convention does not require the United States to allow foreign tax credits for Slovenian Assets Tax paid. Since the United States does not impose taxes on capital, the only capital tax covered by the Convention is the Assets Tax of Slovenia. Thus, although the Article is drafted in a reciprocal manner, its provisions are relevant only for the imposition of the Assets Tax of Slovenia. The explanation which follows will be from the perspective of Slovenia as the taxing State.

The Article provides the general rule in paragraph 4 that, except as provided elsewhere in the Article, capital owned by a resident of a Contracting State may be taxed only by that Contracting State. Thus, in general, Slovenia cannot tax a resident of the United States on capital owned by that resident. Exceptions to this general rule are provided in paragraphs 1, 2 and 3.

Paragraph 1 provides that capital represented by real property (as defined in Article 6 (Income from Real Property (Immovable Property))) which is owned by a U.S. resident and located in Slovenia may be taxed by Slovenia. Under paragraph 2, capital which is represented by personal property which is part of the business property of a permanent establishment maintained by a U.S. resident in Slovenia or pertains to a fixed base maintained in Slovenia by a U.S. resident may be taxed by Slovenia. Paragraph 3 deals with capital represented by ships, aircraft or containers that are owned by a U.S. resident, and are operated in international traffic and with other personal property pertaining to the operation of such ships, aircraft or containers. Under the paragraph, such capital is taxable only in the United States.

Thus, the capital to which each of paragraphs 1, 2 and 3 of the Article relate is subject to taxation in the same manner as is income from such capital under Articles 6 (Income from Real Property (Immovable Property)), 7 (Business Profits), 8 (Shipping and Air Transport) and 13 (Gains) of the Convention.

ARTICLE 29 (ENTRY INTO FORCE)

This Article contains the rules for bringing the Convention into force and giving effect to its provisions.

Paragraph 1

Paragraph 1 provides for the ratification of the Convention by both Contracting States according to their constitutional and statutory requirements. Instruments of ratification shall be exchanged as soon as possible.

In the United States, the process leading to ratification and entry into force is as follows: Once a treaty has been signed by authorized representatives of the two Contracting States, the Department of State sends the treaty to the President who formally transmits it to the Senate for its advice and consent to ratification, which requires approval by two-thirds of the Senators present and voting. Prior to this vote, however, it generally has been the practice for the Senate Committee on Foreign Relations to hold hearings on the treaty and make a recommendation regarding its approval to the full Senate. Both Government and private sector witnesses may testify at these hearings. After receiving the Senate's advice and consent to ratification, the treaty is returned to the President for his signature on the ratification document. The President's signature on the document completes the process in the United States.

Paragraph 2

Paragraph 2 provides that the Convention will enter into force upon the exchange of instruments of ratification. The date on which a treaty enters into force is not necessarily the date on which its provisions take effect. Paragraph 2, therefore, also contains rules that determine when the provisions of the treaty will have effect. Under paragraph 2(a), the Convention will have effect with respect to taxes withheld at source (principally dividends, interest and royalties) for amounts paid or credited on or after the first day of the third month following the date on which the Convention enters into force. For example, if instruments of ratification are exchanged on April 25 of a given year, the withholding rates specified in paragraph 2 of Article 10 (Dividends) would be applicable to any dividends paid or credited on or after July 1 of that year. This rule allows the benefits of the withholding reductions to be put into effect as soon as possible, without waiting until the following year. The delay of two to three months is required to allow sufficient time for withholding agents to be informed about the change in withholding rates. If for some reason a withholding agent withholds at a higher rate than that provided by the Convention (perhaps because it was not able to re-program its computers before the payment is made), a beneficial owner of the income that is a resident of Slovenia may make a claim for refund pursuant to section 1464 of the Code.

For all other taxes, paragraph 2(b) specifies that the Convention will have effect for any taxable year or assessment period beginning on or after January 1 of the year following entry into force.

As discussed under Articles 25 (Mutual Agreement Procedure) and 26 (Exchange of Information and Administrative Assistance), the powers afforded the competent authority under these articles apply retroactively to taxable periods preceding entry into force.

ARTICLE 30 (TERMINATION)

This Convention is to remain in effect indefinitely, unless terminated by one of the Contracting States in accordance with the provisions of Article 30. The Convention may be terminated at any time after the year in which the Convention enters into force. If notice of termination is given, the provisions of the Convention with respect to withholding at source will cease to have effect after the expiration of a period of 6 months beginning with the delivery of notice of termination. For other taxes, the Convention will cease to have effect as of taxable periods beginning after the expiration of this 6 month period.

A treaty performs certain specific and necessary functions regarding information exchange and mutual agreement. In the case of information exchange the treaty's function is to override confidentiality rules relating to taxpayer information. In the case of mutual agreement its function is to allow competent authorities to modify internal law in order to prevent double taxation and tax avoidance. With respect to the effective termination dates for these aspects of the treaty, therefore, if a treaty is terminated as of January 1 of a given year, no otherwise confidential information can be exchanged after that date, regardless of whether the treaty was in force for the taxable year to which the request relates. Similarly, no mutual agreement departing from internal law can be implemented after that date, regardless of the taxable year to which the agreement relates. Therefore, for the competent authorities to be allowed to exchange otherwise confidential information or to reach a mutual agreement that departs from internal law, a treaty must be in force at the time those actions are taken and any existing competent authority agreement ceases to apply.

Article 30 relates only to unilateral termination of the Convention by a Contracting State. Nothing in that Article should be construed as preventing the Contracting States from concluding a new bilateral agreement, subject to ratification, that supersedes, amends or terminates provisions of the Convention without the six-month notification period.

Customary international law observed by the United States and other countries, as reflected in the Vienna Convention on Treaties, allows termination by one Contracting State at any time in the event of a "material breach" of the agreement by the other Contracting State.